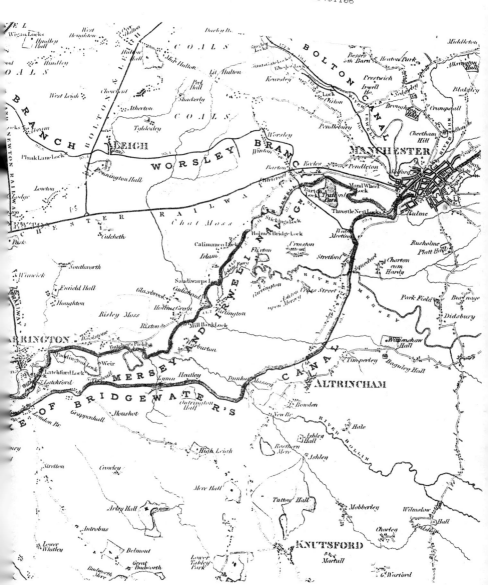

HENRY BOOTH

HENRY BOOTH

INVENTOR — PARTNER IN THE ROCKET
AND
THE FATHER OF RAILWAY MANAGEMENT

Henry Booth

ARTHUR H. STOCKWELL LTD.
Elms Court   Ilfracombe
Devon

ISBN 0 7223 1358-6
Printed in Great Britain by
Arthur H. Stockwell Ltd.
Elms Court   Ilfracombe
Devon

Contents

Illustrations

Preface

A *Memoir of Henry Booth* by Robert Smiles appeared shortly after his death. In his Preface Mr. Smiles wrote that: '. . . Mr. Booth's public services as one of the earliest promoters of railways, and the important part he has performed in the successful practical development of the railway system, are not as generally known, or as well appreciated, as his merits and the value of his services demand. But, further, although Mr. Booth's long and useful public life was mainly devoted to the promotion of railway interests, he was much more than a "Railway Man".'

In 1851 Mr. J. Francis — author of works on the Stock Exchange and the Bank of England — in his *History of English Railways* wrote of Henry Booth at the end of his section on the Liverpool & Manchester Railway: 'He among others, has been termed the founder of modern Locomotion; and the writer has seen sufficient confidently to assert that to this gentleman not only the Liverpool & Manchester, but the entire world of railways, is greatly indebted.'

A more recent writer on the Liverpool & Manchester Railway — an American, Robert E. Carlson (1969) — wrote about Henry Booth: '. . . from the moment he entered the Liverpool and Manchester Railway group he demonstrated an unusual gift for promotional and organizational work; from the beginning he gave new vitality to the project. A skilful organizer with great energy and remarkable administrative ability his value was immediately recognized by the committee, who promptly appointed him their Secretary; when the Liverpool and Manchester Railway Company was chartered, he was made the Treasurer. Booth proved as versatile as he was capable; he wrote two prospectuses and most of the official reports published between 1824 and 1830.'

The *Memoir* by Robert Smiles was written for private circulation and was based principally on a number of articles which he had contributed to the *Railway News*, of which he was the editor, and there is little reference to Henry Booth's work as Manager of the Liverpool & Manchester Railway or as Joint Secretary of the London & North Western Railway. In the Railway Archives at the Public Records Office, Minutes and Reports written by Henry Booth during this period are now accessible, so that it is possible to enlarge upon the work he did which led to safe and efficient railway systems throughout the world.

There are details in the *Memoir* of Henry Booth's publications, but there is no mention of the leading part which he took in the commercial and political life of Liverpool. In the period 1820 to 1830 he was often one of the principal speakers at meetings and his speeches covered a wide range of subjects, many of them showing the same vision of a better world which appears in his published writing.

On the 2nd January 1869, not long before he died, Henry Booth, with his unmarried daughter Mary Anne, attended the christening of Charles, the eldest son of his nephew Alfred Booth. The consequences were that Mary Anne took a special interest in Charles who, in due course, named his eldest son Henry. When she died in 1908 some of her possessions and a number of her papers were passed on to Charles Booth and these are now in the possession of the author.

Note: Quotations throughout are given in their original spelling.

Chapter I

Henry Booth was the eldest son of Thomas Booth (1749-1832) a leading Liverpool merchant. The following excerpts are from a short autobiographical note which he wrote a few years before he died, and which was found with the papers of his unmarried daughter Mary Anne, when she died in 1908.*

'My father, Thomas Booth, was a younger son of a yeoman farmer and small landowner in Orford, a parish or place a few miles from Warrington. When a boy, he was sent to Liverpool by his parents to work out his own fortune, just now a hundred years since, that is to say about 1764. He was fortunate in being bound to a respectable corn-merchant, in whose house he resided. I believe his master's name was Dobson, and that he lived in Clayton Square. There were very few houses in the Square, which at that time was near the outskirts of the Town. According to the maps of that date the top of Church Street was the limit of the town in that direction: Bold Street, with its splendid shops and Lyceum Library, was not in existence, not even marked out in the map; fields and waste ground extended in a south-easterly direction through the site of St. George Square etc., as far as Park Lane, which then stretched out as at present from the old Dock, the site of the present

*The author was present when the note was read aloud at a family gathering on a Sunday afternoon in that year. Much of it was included in *Alfred Booth* by Harriet Anna Whitting and the account is taken from the book.

11

Custom-house, to the Ancient Chapel of Toxteth Park. The population of Liverpool at that date was under 30,000 souls, while at present it is nearly 500,000, but the commerce of the port was thriving. The African Trade, including the Slave Trade, in regard to which Liverpool held a bad pre-eminence, had been established some thirty years, and the records of the time state that seventy-four vessels sailed for Africa in the year 1764. In the following year Gore's first newspaper was published containing fifteen advertisements, and in 1766 the first Liverpool Directory was published in small octave size. Another brother of my father, my uncle George Booth, also settled in Liverpool. The two men were very dissimilar in character. My uncle George was grave and thoughtful, slow in coming to a decision, fond of intricate calculations, whether in matters of account or in mechanical problems. My father was the man of business, prompt, energetic and decisive. They were very many years in partnership, but it will be readily understood that my father took the lead as acting partner, while my uncle generally acquiesced in his proceedings. They respected each other, and, though not demonstrative on either side, were evidently actuated by mutual esteem and regard. When my father's term of apprenticeship had expired, he started on his own account in the same business, and I perceive in the Liverpool Directory for 1774 the record of "Thomas Booth, Corn Factor, 19 King Street". At that early period of the commercial history of Liverpool, a young man of character, energy and ability had probably not much difficulty, though possessing in the way of capital little beyond the personal qualities I have named, in laying the foundation of a tolerably successful career. The last quarter of the eighteenth century was evidently a period of energetic commercial enterprise, especially noted for the establishment of Inland Navigation. In 1774 the first boat was launched in the Leeds and Liverpool Canal. The Duke of Bridgewater's Canal was opened about the same period, and from that date to the close of the century the most important canals in the Kingdom were constructed.

'Having been in business some fourteen years my father probably considered himself in a position to become a family man. About 1785 he married Miss Esther Noble of Lancaster, and brought his bride to his residence in Union Street, at that period a pleasant part of the town near the "Ladies' Walk" and the banks of the Leeds Canal, which stretched for many miles through the open country to the northward of the town. My father had two daughters born to him, my sisters Jane and Esther, before I can presume to lay claim to having made my appearance in the world. Meanwhile trade, I apprehend, continued prosperous, for in four or five years after his marriage he removed to a commodious house, which he built for himself in Rodney Street, an open district at the opposite extremity of the town. I was the eldest son of my parents, and I understand the date when my excellent mother gave birth to her first boy was the 4th April 1789* and in the Liverpool Directory of 1790 I find the name of Thomas Booth at that time residing in Rodney Street.** My scholastic education commenced in good time, for it so happened there was a dame's school of some repute immediately at the back of my father's house, in the ground now forming part of the precincts of St. Luke's Church. At three years old or thereabouts I entered on my literary labours. It was not many years after this epoch, before I was considered sufficiently advanced to be sent to a Boys' School in Duke Street, kept by the Rev. W. Lewin, Minister at Benn's Garden Chapel, situate in an out-of-the-way place leading from Red Cross Street, where my parents, being Presbyterian Dissenters, regularly attended. About the date of my father's marriage seems to have been something of an epoch in the commercial prosperity of the town. In 1785 the first mail coach was established between Liverpool and London. At that date Castle Street, which led directly to the

*Robert Smiles gives the date of Henry Booth's birth as the 4th April 1788, and this has been copied by the *Dictionary of National Biography* and subsequent writers. The inscription on his gravestone states that he died on the 28th March, aged 80 years. 1788 is given as the year of his birth on the memorial tablet in the Ullet Road Unitarian Church and on the statue in St. George's Hall. The census returns for 1861 confirm the 1789 date as being correct; this was taken on the 7th April and Henry Booth gave his age as 72.
**To commemorate the birth there of Henry Booth, the Liverpool Heritage Bureau has placed a plaque on the house at the corner of Rodney Street and Leece Street, now the British Legion Club.

Town Hall, was so narrow that only two carriages could pass one another, but in the following year it was widened, and shortly became the most spacious and important street in the town. In 1786 the Music Hall in Bold Street was opened, an excellent concert room, where for many years Braham, Mrs. Billington, and other vocal celebrities exhibited their talents to delighted audiences. So Liverpool continued to enjoy a prosperous commerce, and in natural sequence to increase rapidly in brick and mortar.'

Henry Booth was then sent to the Rev. Shepherd's Boarding School at Gateacre where there were some twenty boys. Mr. Shepherd was the Minister of the small Unitarian (previously Presbyterian) Chapel there and the claims of his church and congregation absorbed only a limited portion of his time, leaving him free to devote himself to the education of a number of boys. Henry's youngest brother Charles, who went to the school ten years later was very unhappy there, according to the recollection of his daughter Anna.* Mr. Shepherd was apparently considered something of an educational celebrity in Liverpool, but Charles suffered much under his birch rod regime.

The Rev. William Shepherd (1768-1847) was, however, a man who must have inspired his older pupils. His teaching covered science as well as the classics. In 1815, with two other clergymen, he published *Systematic Education*, dealing with the various departments of literature, science and the arts, with practical rules for studying each branch of useful knowledge.** His father (a Freeman or Burgess of Liverpool) died when he was four years old, and when he was ten his mother died and he was brought up by Tatlock Mather, his mother's brother, Minister of the Unitarian Chapel at Rainford, near St. Helens. He was educated at the Academy at Daventry and the New College at Hackney, two of the many establishments which provided higher education for the children of dissenters, who were not admitted to Oxford and Cambridge. Mr. Shepherd came to Liverpool in 1790 to tutor

---

*Married 1857 Philip Holt, one of the founders of the Blue Funnel Line.
**Two thick volumes 8vo, 9 plates £1.11.6d. in boards and further editions were published in 1817 and 1823.

The Rev. William Shepherd

(From a lithograph in the Public Reference Library, Liverpool, of a drawing by J. Dickson)

the children of the Rev. John Yates, Minister of the Ancient
Chapel at Toxteth. In 1791 he became the Minister at
Gateacre, and in that year he married Frances Nicholson, the
daughter of a Liverpool merchant.

The Rev. Shepherd had most influence on Henry Booth as a
result of his activities as a leader of the Reform movement. In
1796 he was admitted a Freeman of the Borough and took an
active part in municipal affairs in the advanced liberal
interest. He was an eloquent speaker, and at most meetings
and dinners of the Reformers, he made the principal speech.
Reporting on a dinner in December 1822, the *Liverpool
Mercury* wrote that: 'The Rev. W. Shepherd presided with the
ability, humour and amenity of manner for which he is so
highly distinguished.' Another instance of his varied interests
— in 1825 at the first annual meeting of the Liverpool
Catholic Association, one of many formed in Lancashire to
promote Catholic Emancipation, Mr. Shepherd was described
as for forty years a friend of the oppressed, and of civil and
religious liberty, and a Mr. M'Dermott paid a well merited
eulogium to him and Mr. William Rathbone for their
advocacy of Catholic Emancipation and the excellence of their
individual characters.

Henry Booth's note continues:

'At this time, at the commencement of the nineteenth
century whilst Liverpool was busy and prosperous, the
political atmosphere was not free from disturbance.
Bonaparte was approaching the zenith of his power; alarm
was felt throughout the country at the mighty preparations
which the great Napoleon was making for the Invasion of
England. Liverpool was loyal as well as prosperous, and her
great merchants showed themselves equal to the occasion.
John Bolton, Esquire, raised a Regiment of Volunteers, of
which he became the Colonel. The Corporation gave their
aid to the general movement, and two other Regiments were
raised, one commanded by Colonel George Williams, an
experienced officer, and the other by Colonel W. Earle.
Government testified approval by sending down His Royal
Highness Prince William Duke of Gloucester, who took up

his residence at St. Domingo House as Commander of the District. So we had mustering of Regiments with Drums and Fifes, parade days and reviews with flying of colours and firing of guns, all which was very agreeable in holiday time in my boyish schooldays.*

'Referring to the early days of this century, when Bonaparte was the object of dread rather than of admiration, and a military spirit was aroused amongst our trading communities, duelling was a marked, though not a favourable sign of the time. In 1804 Mr. Sparling shot and killed Mr. Grayson [a shipbuilder] in a duel and the next year Colonel Bolton [of the 1st. Volunteers] shot Major Brooks [of the 2nd. Battalion]. We may congratulate ourselves that a more enlightened public opinion has put a stop to the barbarous practice of duelling.'

About 1804 Henry Booth left school and entered his father's office, but his tastes lay in different directions; as he himself says: '. . . my taste pretty early showed itself for subjects of Natural Philosophy, Mechanics and Hydraulics.' This liking for mechanics, which dates from his earliest days, is admirably illustrated in a story of Henry Booth's boyhood, told by Smiles in his *Memoir*:

'In the long past days of Mr. Booth's boyhood, Rodney Street, as well as others of even the older streets of Liverpool was not so closely lined with houses as it is now. Mr. Thomas Booth's house had a garden in the rear, and on one side a large vacant space, now built upon, which was used by the children as a playground. Mr. Booth, who seems to have been a kind and wisely indulgent father, took his children to the circus to witness the wonderful exploits of Ducrow, alias Craw, or some other itinerant equestrian of the period. The youngsters were doubtless greatly excited and vastly pleased by the visit, and Henry at once turned it to account. It is not recorded whether the boys held a council on the subject, but

---

*In 1803, on George III's Birthday, there was a grand review of the Liverpool Volunteers which numbered — 1 colonel, 6 lieutenant-colonels, 8 majors, 54 captains, 111 subalterns, 221 sergeants, 152 musicians, and 3,313 rank and file.

the probability is that Henry held office as director of the sports, without election, by virtue of seniority and superior capability. However this may be, he resolved, with the hearty concurrence of his younger brothers, Tom, Charles and James, but without hope of effective assistance from them in the most difficult part of the enterprise, to establish a circus! He undertook, of necessity, at the same time willingly, the conjoined important offices of constructor of the circus, chief saddler, property-man (in theatrical parlance), carriage builder, horse-breaker, master of the horse, with any other administrative offices necessary to be filled in carrying the project into effect. His first piece of work was to mark off and lay down suitably the circus ring, which was situated in the playground before referred to. "Dandy" the docile family pony — a real live pony and a great pet of the boys — had to be broken to the ring, then furnished with a flat-topped saddle, suitable for equestrian performances: this piece of work Henry executed to the entire satisfaction of every member of the troupe. The provision of a long rein, by which "Dandy" could be driven from the centre of the ring, was a bagatelle to the master saddler. The carriage-builder's functions were more difficult and important, including, as they did, the construction of a war-chariot of somewhat similar pattern to those used in the time of Cyrus. But the chariots of Cyrus had probably tolerably straight runs for the greater part, and had never to describe curves as stiff as the periphery of the boys' playground circus. "Dandy" would have had an awkward load indeed, the charioteers would have had a very uncomfortable ride, and the progress of the car round the ring would have been anything but the poetry of motion, if Henry had not been able to adapt the axles to the curve more skilfully and scientifically than is done in the railway carriages of the present day, the rigid rectangular axles of which cause the wheels to grind the rails of the curves round which they pass. The young amateur mechanic solved practically, in so far as the circumstances of "the company" were concerned, the "radial axle" problem, which has engaged so much attention since that time. He so contrived the axles of the circus carriage that they could be adjusted at right angles to the body of the vehicle, for an ordinary straight course, or as perfect radii from the centre of the ring, which gave a true, smooth, and easy motion. We are unable to give particulars as to the nature of the performances; they were probably of a very simple character, as "Dandy" would not be likely to acquire readily, and so perfectly as to make somersaults quite safe, the steady amble of the circus hack.'

'At the age of 20, however, it was the Literary and Social side of life that chiefly interested Henry Booth, and . . . the study of Political Economy, but not before he had made "some tentative efforts at poetry".

'"In 1811," he says, "I published a Poem entitled 'Commerce', and some years later I sent to the press 'Sebastian', a tragedy. Neither of these publications won many laurels for their author, and it was not long before I entertained a strong conviction that poetry was not my forte."

'It was during "the poetical epoch of his life" that he became acquainted with "one of the fair daughters of Mr. and Mrs. Crompton, of Chorley Hall". This was in the spring of 1812.'*

Henry Booth continued:

'It was quite consistent with the unfavourable opinion I always entertained of long courtships, that in the autumn of that year, our local papers announced that on the 12th of August of that year I was married to Ellen, eldest daughter of Abraham Crompton, Esq., of Chorley Hall in this county. It is pretty clear that the great subject of Political Economy and the disputed theories on population, did not then engage much of my attention, and I believe that neither my wife's father nor mine had gone deep into those studies: so on our wedding tour (railways not being then invented) we made the most of a travelling chaise, and in buoyant spirits scampered up the picturesque hills, and through the luxuriant vales of Derbyshire, leaving abstruse theories, whether disputed or otherwise, till a more convenient season.'

*Alfred Booth.

Ellen Crompton was the eldest child of Abraham Crompton (1757-1829) and Alice Hayhurst (1763-1853) who were married in 1788. They had thirteen children born between 1789 and 1806, four sons and nine daughters, of whom the first five were girls. When Abraham died, he was survived by twelve of his children.

Abraham Crompton had several connections with Liverpool. His sister Mary married a second cousin, Peter Crompton, who, when his elder brother died, inherited the family fortune and moved, about 1798, from Derby to Eton,* near Liverpool, where he lived the life of a country gentleman, but being a Doctor of Physic, attended to the needs of the sick poor in the neighbourhood. Like the Rev. Shepherd, Peter Crompton was a leading member of the Reform movement in Liverpool and stood for Parliament in Liverpool and Preston.

Alice Hayhurst was a daughter of a Liverpool West Indian Merchant. He changed his name to France, the name of his uncle, senior partner in the firm, when the uncle died. One of the partners in the firm was Thomas Fletcher, whose daughter Caroline (1805-1882) married Charles Crompton** (1797-1865), son of Peter Crompton. Another daughter, Emily (1803-1853) married Charles Booth (1799-1860), Henry Booth's youngest brother.

Abraham Crompton's eighth daughter Jessy (1801-1890) married Edmund Potter (1802-1883) of Dinting Vale, Glossop, at one time the largest calico printer in the world. Their granddaughter Beatrix Potter (Mrs. W. Heelis) famous for her Peter Rabbit books, recorded in her journal in 1883 about her great grandfather:***

'When Grandmother Potter was young 55 years ago Mr. Crompton brought her and several other daughters down South in his own carriage with four horses. They went to Stoke Poges near Windsor to see the castle. Mr. Crompton was not very particular about his appearance. On this

---

*Near Knotty Ash, now spelt Eaton.
**Later Sir Charles Crompton, a High Court Judge.
***Henry Booth's name, as the husband of Ellen Crompton, appears in the genealogy in the Family Bible kept at Hill Top, Sawry.

occasion he wore a suit of Jane.'*

The Rev. Shepherd and Henry Booth were two of Abraham Crompton's four executors. Mr. Shepherd had, with Alice Crompton, the additional duty of approving the marriage of any of the daughters under twenty-one, before she could receive her dowry of £4,000. Henry Booth was also made trustee of settlements made on Abraham's death on some of his children, and as last surviving executor had much work to do in later years clearing up the Crompton estate.

*The journal's editor, in a footnote, states: 'An undressed cotton material now known as Jean.' Abraham Crompton was thus anticipating the fashion of 150 years later.

Chapter II

Henry Booth first worked in his father's business, but at some stage, before he married, he left his father and started independently as a corn merchant in partnership with Joseph Hancox, who had married his eldest sister Jane, the office being in Bank Buildings, Castle Street. At this time, he was also agent in Liverpool for the Albion Fire and Life Insurance Company. On the 29th September 1812 a formal notice in the *Liverpool Mercury* announced that Henry Booth and Joseph Hancox had dissolved their partnership by mutual consent, and for the next six months Joseph Hancox acted as agent for the Insurance Company. However, in an advertisement concerning the renewal of Insurance Policies at the March Quarter Day 1813, the Agents were described as Hancox, Booth and M'Kune and this firm continued as agents until September 1816 when Henry Booth's younger brother George became the agent. Thomas M'Kune appears in the Liverpool Directory of 1818 as a corn merchant living at 45 Great George Street with premises at 6 Wapping. Henry Booth is described as a merchant in all the directories and his address is given as 10 Lodge Lane; it is given as Nile Street, presumably a business address, in the 1812 and 1818 election records. His business appears to have been on a small scale and from all accounts was not very successful.

At this period Henry Booth was far more interested in politics, mechanics and philosophy. One of his first publications was a paper entitled 'Suggestions concerning

Moral Capability' which he read to the Literary and Philosophical Society in Liverpool in 1813, and which was published in the *Monthly Repository of Theology and General Literature* in February 1814. The *Monthly Repository* was a theological magazine '. . . which is open to free and at the same time temperate discussion, which avows and cherishes the Protestant principle with the Bible and the Bible only as the standard and authority of revealed religion.' In the January number the editor had added to this statement the comment that the New Year was about to set in auspiciously and that the return of peace was likely. This magazine was distributed widely by Unitarian organizations throughout the country. However, some years later, it was considered too subversive as reading matter for the prisoners by the Governor of Lancaster Prison, and he was later supported in his objections by the magistrates, and subsequently by quarter sessions.

Of the Literary and Philosophical Society of Liverpool, Thomas Fletcher wrote in his autobiography, written in 1843:

'Towards the end of the year 1813, I became a member of the Literary and Philosophical Society, then first established; at all events I was an original member. The Rev. Theophilus Houlbrooke, then residing at Green Bank, was the first President, and T. Stewart Traill M.D. now Professor of Medical Jurisprudence in the University of Edinburgh, the Secretary. When Mr. Houlbrooke went to live near London, Mr. William Roscoe was appointed President and on his death, Dr. Traill . . . succeeded him. Its meetings were held monthly during the winter months, when papers on Scientific and Literary subjects were read; after which there was a conversation for the rest of the evening . . . . This Society still continues to exist and of late has assumed somewhat of a popular character by opening its doors to meetings of a more general cast, denominated Soirees.'

Henry Booth's lecture represented the thoughts of a young man, brought up in a family of traditional but advanced religious views, with a knowledge and interest in recent scientific discoveries, attempting to get some satisfactory explanation of the purpose of life. The problem of predestination and of the free agency of man was the basic subject; that man has the power to improve the capacities nature has given him:

> 'That the Deity is all powerful is admitted — that he can control the events of the world is allowed; but the power which is possessed is not always exerted, God having bestowed upon his creatures a nature suitable for his purposes, may for their good decline to influence the general tenor of their actions before they are performed. . . A vessel in a strong current cannot be prevented from going with the stream, but a skilful pilot may frequently chuse the line of his course and avoid the rocks he cannot remove.'

At that period, however, politics were becoming a major interest in Liverpool, which had been a Borough sending two members to Parliament since 1207, during the reign of King John. In 1815 it was the only large town in England where, due to the growth of commerce and industry, the population was increasing rapidly, which was represented in Parliament. Birmingham, Manchester, Leeds and Sheffield, other growing industrial towns, were not represented in Parliament. In consequence, the elections in Liverpool in the earlier part of the nineteenth century were of increasing importance and attracted attention throughout the country.

Thomas Booth took an active part in politics, because he was a Freeman. He and his brother George became Freemen, because they had served an apprenticeship with one, which was the most common way of newcomers to the town becoming Burgesses. Sons of Freemen were entitled to become Freemen and, in due course, Thomas Booth's five sons were Freemen.

Before the reforms of 1835, the Freemen of Liverpool owned all the municipal property, were the only people eligible to vote in the elections for Members of Parliament or for the Mayor and Bailiffs (the officers who enforced the regulations of the Council), to be members of the Council or to hold any office in the Borough. Freemen were exempt from the payment of town dues or goods imported into the town and had only to pay half the tolls due in the market.* The Mayor could appoint one Freeman after his year of office and in earlier days, the Council sold the right to become a Freeman, but in 1777 the Council passed a resolution to stop this practice. As a result, a large body of the leading merchants who were newcomers to the town could take no part in municipal affairs, and, in addition, had to pay the town dues and full market tolls. With a population which doubled between 1801 and 1831, the number of Freemen remained constant at just under 4,000.** One reason for the Council not adding to the number of Freemen was the potential loss of revenue if the number of merchant and trader Freemen was increased. The other was the constitution of the Council dating back to the Charter of William III in 1695. The Council appointed its own members for life (although for non-attendance or some misdemeanour they could be removed) and only the Mayor and the two Bailiffs were elected by the Freemen. The Charter was badly drafted and vague and although attempts were made to alter the situation the Council retained its powers, because it could afford to continue litigation until those opposing it ran out of funds. This peculiar composition and constitution of the Council caused resentment, and was also an important reason for the opposition of the Council to the Liverpool & Manchester Railway Bill in 1825.

Thomas Booth played a prominent part in the election in 1806 when the Reform party managed to elect Mr. William Roscoe to Parliament, unseating General Tarleton, who had been a Member since 1790, but in the next election in 1807 General Tarleton regained the seat at the expense of Mr. Roscoe.*** On the 8th November 1811 there was a dinner at the York Hotel to celebrate the fifth anniversary of Mr.

---

*In 1832 town dues produced £22,000 and the market tolls £11,000 after expenses.
**Ramsay Muir. However, in the election in November 1830 caused by Mr. Huskisson's death, 4,401 actually voted and 897 are listed as not having done so.
***In 1812 just before the next election, an advertisement appeared in the *Liverpool Mercury* calling for a meeting of Freemen who had not been paid the sums promised by the Generals; because General Tarleton still owed money he only received 11 votes in that election.

Roscoe's election, the Rev. Shepherd in the chair, dinner on the table at 4 p.m. After the toast to Mr. Roscoe, of the personal toasts drunk that evening, that to the health of Mr. Thomas Booth followed the one to Mr. Roscoe.

In 1813 the Reformers in Liverpool started the Concentric Society, the first President being Colonel George Williams of the 2nd Volunteer Regiment, and it is clear that Henry Booth belonged to the Society. It had weekly meetings in the evening, a dinner every quarter and an anniversary dinner in December to commemorate its first meeting. At the anniversary dinner in December 1818, the Rev. Shepherd presided. The principal guest was Sir Francis Burdett, one of the Members of Parliament for Westminster.* There were three hundred guests at the dinner, which started at 5.30 p.m. and did not end until midnight. Numerous toasts were drunk and to quote the *Liverpool Mercury*: 'When the toast of the Lancashire Witches** was given out, all eyes were naturally bent on to the orchestra, where was observed a display of female taste and beauty.' Mr. Shepherd gave the toast to Colonel Williams: '. . . the gallant soldier who had beaten his sword into a ploughshare.' He then gave details of the Concentric Society for the benefit of the visitors. It was founded at the end of 1812, after Mr. Henry Brougham had been defeated in the election, due to the need for a rallying point, and with the object of uniting all classes of Reformers. In his speech, which covered a wide range of subjects, he made a remark with which Henry Booth did not agree, and as a result of this a letter from him appeared in the next week's *Liverpool Mercury*. The letter he wrote is dealt with later in this chapter.

After various speeches, Mr. Ryley, the 'Honorary Songsmith' of the Society, sang, and those present were asked: '. . . to assist in the chorus with as much energy as they conceived the sentiments merited.' The final speech was by Mr. Egerton Smith, the proprietor and editor of the *Liverpool Mercury*.

At the anniversary dinner in 1819 one of the toasts drunk was to: '. . . our venerable friend Abraham Crompton of Lune

---

*One of the few Boroughs where all householders of £10 rateable value had a vote.
**Lancashire Witch — a young lady or girl of bewitching appearance and manners.

Villa', (Skirton near Lancaster) where he had moved on selling Chorley Hall.

After 1823 the Concentric Society disappears from the columns of the *Liverpool Mercury*. The reason was the advent of a more progressive Member of Parliament in February 1823, William Huskisson, who was elected in the place of George Canning, when he was appointed Governor General of India.*

Henry Booth and his brothers James and Thomas took an active part in the election of 1818 when Lord Sefton stood for the Reform movement against the Rt. Hon. George Canning and General Gascoyne. Much work had to be done because many potential Freemen, who had served apprenticeships in various skilled trades, did not register until an election came along, when they expected one of the candidates to pay the fee — £2 (half of which was a perquisite of the Town Clerk). When the election was due, the candidates entertained their supporters in a lavish way, vast quantities of drink were consumed and it was then important to make sure that the voter went into the right booth. The supporters of Lord Sefton, who received 1,207 votes at his booth, were very successful in persuading 1,086 Freemen not to vote for the other two candidates. Canning received 103 and Gascoyne only 55 plumpers. The final totals were:

Rt. Hon. George Canning	1,651 votes
General Gascoyne	1,444 votes
Lord Sefton	1,287 votes

There was an election dinner on the 6th July, and among the toasts drunk was one to the helpers in the election, the Croppers, the Rathbones, the Booths, and another to Charles Lawrence and the election committee, all names to be met with later in connection with the Liverpool & Manchester Railway.

Thomas Fletcher wrote of 1820 in his autobiography:

'. . . the remarkable circumstance in this year was the

---

*Canning never left for India, because just before his departure, Castlereagh, Lord Londonderry, the Foreign Minister, committed suicide and Canning was appointed to this office.

return of the Queen (Caroline), wife of George IV., after a
long absence from England, and her trial before the House
of Lords with a view of degrading her from her rank by Act
of Parliament; a proceeding which it is well known was
abandoned by Lord Liverpool's ministry although they had
a majority of the House against her. But such was the
excitement of the public mind that the Government
withdrew the bill. . . . After her virtual acquittal there was a
public meeting in Liverpool for an address to her, as was the
case indeed throughout the kingdom. . . . There was also a
procession in Liverpool to celebrate the event, such a
procession as was never seen before. It was two or three
miles long,* and consisted of all sorts of people of the town
and neighbourhood. . . . There was a shilling subscription
set on foot in Liverpool to present her with a piece of plate,
to which I gave my mite, but she did not live to receive it.'

The first of Henry Booth's speeches to be reported in the
Liverpool Mercury, was at a grand dinner of the Friends of
Liberty and Law at the York Hotel on the 20th November
1820, to celebrate the termination of the unconstitutional
proceedings against the Queen in the House of Lords. Thomas
Booth was in the chair, supported on his right by Mr. Joseph
Birch, Member of Parliament for Nottingham, and the
vice-chairman was Colonel Williams. The stewards included
several future directors of the Liverpool & Manchester
Railway, Lister Ellis, Charles Lawrence, William Rathbone
and Joseph Sandars. The *Liverpool Mercury* reported that:
'The dinner was very superb, the game abundant and the wine
of fine flavour. When the cloth was withdrawn the following
toasts were given with great enthusiasm, The King, The Queen
(three times three, thrice repeated).' There were many other
toasts, finally to the Town and Trade of Liverpool and the
Lancashire Witches. Then, after a short speech by Thomas
Booth, the *Liverpool Mercury* reported as follows:

'Mr. Henry Booth, in a very feeling and eloquent address,
complimented the generous devotion of the people, who

*The *Liverpool Mercury* estimated the length at 8,368 yards.

proved themselves capable of throwing the broad shield of protection over insulted innocence. He congratulated the people on the present occasion, as they had hitherto few opportunities of meeting to celebrate anything favourable to their country; the people had nobly fought and nobly won the late arduous battle. This was a lesson to ministers for daring to trample upon the best interests of the nation, and the most honourable affections of the human heart. . . . The enlightened spirit of the people was honourably opposed to the corrupt influence which unfortunately pervades even the Lords and Commons of this country. He hoped all would join in concord; for a necessity might soon arise when all should unite to call for punishment upon the authors of the late disgraceful conspiracy, when he trusted that every man would extend the right hand of fellowship upon the occasion and be at his post.'

After further speeches and drinking of toasts, amongst which was the health of the Earl of Sefton: 'Mr. Ryley gave several of his comic songs with great effect, particularly a new one written for the occasion . . . the greatest hilarity prevailed throughout the evening, and the company separated a little before midnight, highly delighted with the festivities of the day.'

In 1818 Henry Booth published a pamphlet entitled 'The Question of the Poor Laws'. The full title was much longer and ended 'the laws and principles of Population briefly explored and illustrated'. As mentioned previously, he had taken exception to some remarks made by the Rev. Shepherd at the Concentric Society dinner in December of that year, and had written to the *Liverpool Mercury* on the subject. The remarks to which he objected were quoted in his letter, which was headed 'To the Rev. W. Shepherd':

'The condition of the labouring classes in this kingdom has given rise to the most cold blooded speculations, and preparations are evidently making to ripen these speculations into practice. — Woe be to him that shall say to this class of the community, — follow not the dictates of nature — comply not with the law of the Almighty — propagate not your species; or if you do, do it at the peril of starving, together with your offspring!'

After this extract from Mr. Shepherd's speech, the letter continues:

'In this clause, you renounce all pretensions to argument; and appealing alone to the passions and prejudices of your audience, you hurl your anathema against every man who, . . . is so unfortunate as to differ from yourself.'

Henry Booth then refers to his pamphlet:

'I have lately, in a short publication upon the question of the Poor Laws, expressed myself very unequivocally on this subject, as the direct advocate of that principle which you have thought proper, ex cathedra, very summarily to denounce. I shall therefore entreat your permission to offer very briefly, a few suggestions for your deliberate consideration.
    'In the higher and middle classes of society, is there not practised to a very considerable degree, that prudence and precaution on the subject of marriage, the reasonableness of which the advocates of limitation and moral restraint are anxious to impress upon the minds of the poor?'

The very long letter then drew attention to a number of the facts which were in the pamphlet. In large towns, half the population died before reaching the age of manhood, and that the best way to reduce this mortality would be by reducing the number of births, so that a smaller number of children could be brought up to live a healthy and satisfying life. The death of children in their early years was due to overcrowding, disease and malnutrition; there would be an outcry if sheep or horses died off like humans. Where conditions were favourable, as in America, the population had increased rapidly in the last thirty years, and if the same increase of population had occurred in England, the population in 1818 would have been 192 million instead of 10 million. Even with the greatest possible improvements in domestic agriculture, the maximum population which could have been supported would have been only 15 million.

In the pamphlet Henry Booth points out that the assistance given by poor relief actually aggravated rather than alleviated the problem, as parents were enabled to have more children. Poor relief in Lancashire had increased eight times to nearly half a million pounds annually in forty years, and some better way was needed to deal with the problem of over population. His view was that early marriages, where a family would not be supported adequately, should be discouraged. He did not advocate legislation as every case was different, but that a new dimension should be given to public opinion. Hitherto the idea had been inculcated that fathering a large family was patriotic, but there was no honour in having a large family unless it could be brought up in comfort. This doctrine should be instilled into everyone and in all public institutions, posted in schools as a leading principle and duty, and enforced from the pulpit and made explicit in the marriage service. Someone might say: "What! is the rich man to marry when he pleases and must the poor man be debarred this one solace in his misfortunes? . . . I wish to save him from avoidable misfortune, discourage unwise marriages which bring misery and expense upon the nation."

In a lecture which he gave in Liverpool in 1860, after he had retired, he pointed out that in spite of all the great advances during the previous forty years, poverty was still as prevalent as ever. As a result of further research into the subject, he found that in various countries the population was controlled by law, and quoted the cases of Norway and Wurttemberg. In Norway, marriage in agricultural areas was not permitted until the young man owned a farm. In Wurttemberg, no man was allowed to marry before he was twenty-five, on account of military service, and then he had to produce evidence of ability to support a family before marrying — similar conditions prevailed in Bavaria and Lubeck. He envisaged a better world resulting from a reduced birthrate. 'When no more inhabitants shall be ushered on the threshold of life than there is room for . . . when the poorest labourer may apply himself to his occupation in full feelings of satisfaction and confidence, as he breathes the fresh air of health and liberty may give God thanks for his existence.'

Charles Booth's* interests in the problems of poverty derived
from his uncle's work on the subject, but in his case he devoted
the greater part of his life to investigating the causes of
poverty, rather than looking for panaceas. After his death a
chair in Social Science was endowed at Liverpool University in
memory of Charles Booth. The first Professor, A.M.
Carr-Saunders,** in his book *The Population Problem*,
demonstrated that throughout history in all societies, one of
the means by which the population was kept constant was by
the postponement of marriage.

Steamboats had been introduced on the River Mersey in
1815, and Henry Booth turned his mind to the problems of
steam engines. In 1819 he took out his first patent (No. 4367)
for propelling canal boats, by means of a reciprocating frame
with hinged boards inside the boat. The method would not
have been efficient, but the way in which the power of a steam
engine was to be applied, was by hydraulic transmission, water
or other fluid, in a tube communicating the motion of one
piston to the other.

He became a part owner in the first steamship to carry
passengers from Liverpool to Bagillt on the Dee in North
Wales. The *Liverpool Mercury* reported on the 1st June 1821
that: '. . . the steam packet *Cambria* would start the service
next week'.***

In 1810 the congregation of Benn's Garden Chapel decided
to replace it with a new chapel in Renshaw Street. Benn's

---

*Rt. Hon. Charles Booth, PC. (1840-1916) author of *Life and Labour of the
People in London*.
**Later Sir Alexander Carr-Saunders, Director of the London School of
Economics.
***On the 8th June an advertisement appeared announcing that the Cambria
would depart from Bagillt at 8 a.m. and leave Liverpool at 4 p.m. calling at
Hoylake to land and embark passengers, every day except Saturdays and
Sundays. On Saturdays the *Cambria* would depart from Bagillt at 7 a.m.
returning to Bagillt to leave for Liverpool again at 5 p.m. returning on Sunday
morning at 8 a.m.

Fares: Best Cabin 3/6 to Hoylake 2/6
Steerage   2/- "   "   1/-
Horses 5/- Gigs 7/6 or together 10/-
4 Wheelers 1 guinea
Sails from St. George's Dock, Pierhead.

Garden could not be approached by carriages and the chapel was no longer in the residential part of the town, which was rapidly spreading outwards. Thomas Booth and his brother George were amongst those who contributed towards the cost, and Renshaw Street Chapel was opened on the 20th October 1811. About 1822 Henry Booth was consulted about heating the chapel, and in their minutes of the 27th January 1823 the chapel committee expressed their thanks for the ingenious method adopted by him for so successfully warming the chapel, and for his great personal attention in carrying it into effect.

Chapter III

Robert Smiles wrote in the *Memoir*: 'Mr. Henry Booth was of a nature and temperament that would not permit him to live in close contact with a felt grievance and injustice without strenuous and persistent protest and remonstrance against it. . . .' His speeches, and his writings, exhibited what Smiles described as a rich vein of dry humour. He spoke at a number of meetings dealing with grievances; he was usually one of the principal speakers, especially when the subject needed study to master all the facts. His speech at a meeting in 1821 to protest against the extension of government controlled bonded warehouses in Liverpool, also illustrates his particular sense of humour.

During the Napoleonic Wars, duties on imported goods had been increased to provide revenue and had reached such levels that the government had agreed to collect the duties only when the goods were sold. While the government had had a tobacco warehouse for many years, arrangements had then to be made for more and more privately owned warehouses to be used to hold goods in bond, once a check had been made to see that they were secure and properly guarded. After a commission of enquiry had reported, the government in 1821 revived a plan to build a complete new set of bonded warehouses in an enclosed area of the docks. The suggestion came when trade was bad and the existing warehouses not fully used, and as a result the Mayor called a meeting in the Town Hall for Thursday, the 7th June 1821. Under the heading: 'Public Meeting on the subject of the proposed scheme of erecting inclosed Warehouses at the Docks, for Bonded Goods', the *Liverpool Mercury* reported on the 8th June: 'Yesterday, at one o'clock, one of the most respectable meetings ever known in Liverpool was held . . . on the above subject, the Worshipful the Mayor in the Chair. It appeared to us that almost every merchant in Liverpool was present . . .'

'A string of resolutions' were proposed by Mr. Alderman Hollinshead* and seconded by Mr. J.B. Yates.** The resolutions having been passed unanimously, Mr. Moses Benson 'read the memorial, which he moved should be carried.'

Henry Booth then said:

'Mr. Mayor, in rising to second the memorial which has just been read, I shall hazard a few remarks upon the reports which have so often been alluded to.

'The several reports of the Commissioners of Inquiry exhibit very curious specimens of argumentation. The 7th of these reports . . . expressly admits, that under a system of exclusive privileges to particular warehouses, the merchant is not able to warehouse his goods upon as advantageous terms as he could do under a system of an open competition. And yet this admission is followed up on the 9th report by recommending that the merchants of Liverpool should be subjected (for their particular accommodation and convenience) to a warehousing scheme, so exclusive in its character, that all competition would be destroyed, and his own warehouses abandoned.

'The 9th report tells us that no warehouse in Liverpool is licensed until it has been regularly surveyed, and declared by the inspecting officer to be "sufficiently secure". It also states that the Department of Warehouse Surveyors, in Liverpool, has of late been conducted with increased vigilance; and that they . . . have no positive proof of any instances in which goods have been improperly removed. Therefore, they humbly submit, to the Lords of the Treasury, that the Liverpool warehouses are *not* sufficiently

---

*A senior Alderman, Mayor in 1807.
**A partner of Thomas Fletcher.

secure, that goods *are* improperly removed, and that the whole system, scheme, and execution, are defective and bad.

'These Commissioners of Inquiry insist, very strenuously, upon the advantages of the warehousing system; and, therefore, in the way of illustration I suppose. . . . it is submitted that the merchant, in "very special cases", may be allowed not to take advantage of these advantages; but may be permitted, as a particular favour, to pay the duties, ex ship upon the landing of the goods; and having so paid every farthing that can possibly be demanded of him he may be graciously allowed to take his own property into his own keeping.

'This is the same, Sir, as if a merchant were to say to a grocer, "You have bought from me twenty hogshead of sugar. It is a great accommodation to you to be allowed two months credit; *therefore*, in 'this very special case', and as a mark of my particular regard, I will allow you to bring me the cash down without discount; and having so paid me for every pound of sugar you have purchased you shall be allowed to remove your sugar to your own premises, and we will say nothing about the two months."

'One thing is remarkable about these reports which is this, such part as relates to Liverpool professes to be drawn up under the sanction of two intelligent Liverpool gentlemen, on the part of the mercantile interest. As I am not aware of any delegation of power either to approve or object to this 9th report, I shall take it for granted there has been some misunderstanding or mistake. One thing is important; that the proceedings of this meeting should make it clear that the town of Liverpool is not pledged either to the doctrine or the logic of these notable reports.

'Sir, it is with this subject as with many others, a plain question seems to be purposely involved in a cloud of technical obscurities. We are told over and over again of the benefits of the bonding system: but who reaps these benefits? It is not so much the merchant as the Exchequer. The bonding system is part of the tactics of the Treasury, for without it the present enormous duties could never be collected. But will anyone say it is for the advantage of commerce that these high duties are imposed? The merchant imports his tobacco at 6d. per pound; the Treasury make a claim of 4s. for every pound before it is allowed to go into consumption. The merchant imports his rum at 20d. per gallon; the Customs demand 12s. for every gallon before it can be used. The capital of our merchants, great as it is, is quite inadequate to satisfy such large demands. The goods, therefore, are put under the King's locks till a third party comes into action, viz. the consumer; who takes them away, little by little, and pays the duty at the same time.

'With respect to the question under our immediate discussion, viz. the proposed alteration of the warehousing system, at Liverpool; or, in the words of the report, the gradual abandonment of our present warehouses, and the building of new ones. What is the plain state of the argument between the Treasury and the merchant, as expounded by these Commissioners of Inquiry? Sir, I conceive it amounts to this: the Treasury say to the merchant, "You are a very useful member of society; for it is in a great measure owing to your enterprize, and skill, and industry, that this country has attained its present rank amongst the nations. You import every variety of produce, from every country in the world; and you have built for yourself large and substantial warehouses, for the convenient storing of your merchandise; an important part of your capital has been so invested with the increasing trade of the port, that these warehouses have necessarily multiplied. . . . The duties, however, which we now call upon you to pay are so heavy. . . . that it is quite impossible you can pay them upon the landing of your goods, therefore, we can no longer allow you to put your own property into your own warehouses. You must remove your sugars, your cottons, your coffees, and your rums, from your own premises and send them to the prison docks, where they shall be so well secured with patent locks, and bolts, and bars, and gates, and walls, that you will have some difficulty in even getting a sight of them again." . . . Circumstanced as this country is at present — having to compete with the whole world, it is more than ever necessary that no artificial vexatious obstructions should impede the enterprise of our merchants. We do not ask for assistance in money, in ships, or in warehouses; but we do ask for every facility in matters of fiscal regulation, to the utmost limits that fair and reasonable security to the revenue will allow. Our prayer is reasonable, and therefore, I cannot for a moment admit that it will be denied.'

The memorial was then put to the meeting and was unanimously carried.

At the beginning of 1822 a movement was started to send an address of congratulation to Mr. Joseph Hume MP who, in the current Parliament, had shown that an active member could, on his own, do effective work in challenging the extravagances and corruptions of government. Joseph Hume (1777-1855) was the son of a sea captain from Montrose in Scotland and was apprenticed at thirteen to a local surgeon and studied medicine at Aberdeen, Edinburgh and London. In 1797 he was appointed an assistant surgeon in the East India Company. After several voyages to India, during one of which the purser died and Hume took over his duties, he was transferred to the land service in India. He became expert in the local languages and was employed on political duties. In 1801 at the start of the Mahratta War, Hume joined the army as a surgeon and interpreter. He was made Paymaster to the Forces and put in charge of the commissariat. In 1807 he retired and returned to England, having amassed a fortune of £40,000 during his service in India. He travelled extensively both in Great Britain and in the Mediterranean, and in 1818 he was elected to Parliament for the Scottish Border Boroughs and remained a Member of Parliament for various constituencies, with one short break, until his death. For over thirty years Joseph Hume was a leader of the Radical party in Parliament and was indefatigable at exposing every kind of extravagance, being an expert on financial questions. Hume made innumerable speeches in Parliament; he spoke at greater length and more often than any other private member of the time, and employed a staff of clerks to assist him in his work.

A meeting to discuss the address to Mr. Hume was held at the Saddle Inn on the 7th January. Henry Booth was present and said that if the Mayor would agree, a meeting should be held in the Town Hall. A year ago a meeting called by the Mayor had resulted in disorder. If this could be avoided by having 'a free and not a packed meeting it would certainly be best' for it to be at the Town Hall.

Henry Booth was referring to a meeting held in December 1820 to consider a loyal address to King George IV on his accession. This had been held at midday in the Court Room at the Town Hall, which could hold eight hundred people at most. When the general public arrived for the meeting, it was found that certain Tory firms had sent all their staff in advance and that the Court Room was full. When the Mayor arrived, he allowed ten Reformers, ten Tories and seven gentlemen of the press to go in with him. After Thomas Booth had made a speech, and the Rev. William Shepherd was speaking, it became clear that the meeting could not continue, owing to the pressure of the people inside and outside the Court Room, and the meeting was abandoned.

In 1822, when a deputation went to the Mayor, he refused to call a public meeting and, in consequence, the promoters organized a meeting to be held in the great room of the York Hotel on Wednesday, the 23rd January. The proposal that Mr. Thomas Booth should occupy the chair was carried with acclamation. He said a few words, after which Colonel Williams proposed the address to Mr. Hume, and spoke at some length detailing the remarkable exposures which Mr. Hume had been able to make of extravagances in the army. Henry Booth seconded the resolution and according to the report in the *Liverpool Mercury*, he said:

'After Colonel Williams' speech, I will not take up too much of your time. I will, however, hazard a few remarks. First, I may congratulate you, that our object is neither to petition or to complain; we have a more pleasing duty to perform. Mr Hume has exhibited what may be accomplished for the public good by individual persevering exertion; it is our part, therefore, to second these exertions, and to give an efficacy of that perseverance by the most important of sanctions, the public approbation. When Mr. Hume started his investigations he was strenuously opposed, thwarted and ridiculed, but he was not put down. It has been the tactics of ministers to render their documents of the public expenditure, voluminous and perplexing. It was insinuated that it was folly for any MP to attempt to unravel the intricacy of their confusion. He was not deterred; he attacked corruption in its strongholds; he has exposed to daylight the deep rooted prodigality of men, who style themselves the government of the country. The people begin to be distrustful of what are termed skilled financiers and they are fast approximating to the opinion of a very sensible writer: "That the best possible system of finance is to spend little; and the best of all taxes, that which is smallest in amount". . . . Gentlemen, it is upon public grounds as an enemy of corruption in all her thousand shapes as well as out of respect to the conduct and character of Mr. Hume, that I join you cordially in the proceedings of this day. I take leave to second the resolution Colonel Williams has proposed.'

The Chairman put the resolution to the meeting and it was carried unanimously. There followed some discussion as to how best to get the Address signed, and Mr. J. Smith* of the *Liverpool Mercury* said the Address would be available for signing at the *Mercury* office on Friday morning.

In May 1824 there was a public meeting in the Town Hall presided over by the Mayor** to pass resolutions in favour of the Government recognizing the New State in South America. Henry Booth moved the second resolution, after having pointed out that there would be little difference of opinion on the importance of trade with South America being placed on a solid and permanent basis. He ended his speech with a plea that higher views than commerce should have their attention, saying:

'Citizens of a free country, whose ancestors bled for their dearest rights, we now come forward to declare our sympathy with nations, who have themselves fought and

*A Partner, but no relation to Mr. Egerton Smith.
**In 1824 the Mayor was Charles Lawrence, who became Chairman of the Liverpool & Manchester Railway.

conquered in the same cause. If England was pre-eminent in commerce and manufacturing enterprise, it was also fitting she should stand foremost as a champion of civil and religious freedom. Let it be her ambition to combine commercial greatness with moral and political superiority; then would her riches and her power be subservient to the noblest ends. She would be hailed as the sanctuary of high and honourable feelings; she would be regarded as the proud beacon of liberty, towering above the darkness and dangers of surrounding despotism, and throwing a burning and shining light to the furthest corners of the globe.'*

It was in this year that Henry Booth joined the new (second) committee of the Liverpool & Manchester Railway. Thomas Booth had been a member of the first committee, and it is usually assumed that Henry replaced his father, then 74, on the new one.

The first project for a railway from Liverpool to Manchester was based on a plan of William James, a solicitor, colliery proprietor and land surveyor and prophet of railways. He interested Joseph Sandars, a leading Liverpool corn merchant and a member of the Reform party in his proposal. Sandars found money for a preliminary survey of the route and formed committees in Liverpool and Manchester, and James was commissioned to make a survey** of the line with a view to promoting a Bill in Parliament.

James was always promising that his surveys would be ready, but they were never completed. He got into financial difficulties in 1823 and spent some time in a debtors prison in that year, and the fact that he had too many interests was further cause for the delay. The result was that no Bill could be prepared for the 1824 Session of Parliament. In 1824 Sandars published a pamphlet on 'The Proposed Rail Road between Liverpool and Manchester, pointing out the necessity for the adoption and the advantages it offers the public', and got the signatures of some one hundred and fifty of the most respectable merchants of Liverpool to a Declaration of

*The *Liverpool Mercury* 11/6/1824.
**One of William James's assistants in this survey was the young Robert Stephenson.

Support. If the project was to succeed, someone of ability was required to provide the driving force and prepared to devote himself fully to it, and Henry Booth, whose activities were well known to Sandars, was the obvious choice and he became Honorary Secretary to the new committee.

Henry Booth, therefore, joined the deputation consisting of Joseph Sandars, Lister Ellis, and John Kennedy of Manchester, which in 1824 visited the various railways working and under construction in the North-East of England. Henry Booth came back convinced that the steam locomotive and railways would revolutionize transport in England and world wide, a view he shared with George Stephenson.

On the return of the deputation, the committee reported on the 20th May 1824 to a meeting of which John Moss was Chairman, when it was resolved to form a 'Company of Proprietors for the establishment of a double Railway between Liverpool and Manchester'. A subscription list was opened and speedily filled and a permanent committee appointed, and Charles Lawrence was elected Chairman. Charles Lawrence had proved a very efficient Mayor, and it was also hoped that he would be able to influence his colleagues on the Council in favour of the railway.

The first step taken by the new committee was to appoint an engineer. When visiting the North-East, Joseph Sandars had met George Stephenson, who was completing his work on the Stockton & Darlington Railway, and had been favourably impressed with the energy and ability that he had shown on that railway. In consequence, on the recommendation of Sandars, the committee appointed George Stephenson as the Engineer.

Henry Booth was principally engaged in collecting facts and figures for the prospectus. After this had been approved by the committee, it was published on the 29th October 1824. The estimated cost of the undertaking was £400,000, including the charge for locomotive engines. The advantage of the railroad compared with the canals, was that goods would take only four to five hours against thirty-six hours in transit from Liverpool to Manchester, and the charges would be reduced by at least one third. There was a need for competition, as owing to their monopoly, the canals overcharged the public. In addition, pilferage, which was facilitated by the circuitous and slow passage by canal, would be reduced. Coal and agricultural produce would be transported more cheaply.

The Bill was presented to Parliament on the 25th February 1825, and a number of members of the committee, one of whom was Henry Booth, were in attendance. There was strong opposition, particularly from the canal companies and the Liverpool Corporation; the general public was also prejudiced against the use of steam locomotives, in view of its experience with steamships in the Mersey belching forth vast amounts of black smoke; this also occurred with the boilers of steam engines driving factory plant or pumps.

On the 15th July 1825, after the failure of the Bill, the *Liverpool Mercury* reporting that a further application to Parliament was planned, commented that:

'. . . while in favour of railways in general, they had never been reconciled to the use of locomotives. Apart from the nuisance from the disgorgement of so many smoking "volcanoes" traversing the country in all directions, they were decidedly of the opinion that the business would be better, more expeditiously and more safely performed by horses.'

The Bill spent thirty-seven days in committee in the House of Commons and then the Preamble was carried by only 37 to 36 votes. On the 1st June the first clause empowering the Company to make the railway was lost by 19 votes to 13. The clause to take land, when put to the vote, was also lost, whereupon Mr. Adam, Counsel for the Railway Company, withdrew the Bill.

What had weakened the case for the railway were serious errors in the survey and the bad impression made by George Stephenson as a witness under cross examination, and his strong Northumberland accent was difficult to understand. The errors of George Stephenson's assistants remained unnoticed until the opposition drew attention to them in committee. Robert Stephenson, who had assisted his father in the survey of the Stockton & Darlington Railway, had decided to take a job with a mining company in South America, and had left England in June 1824.

On the 5th June, twenty-one Members of Parliament met

the Railway Committee at the Royal Hotel in St. James's Street, London, with General Gascoyne in the chair. He was one of Liverpool's two Members of Parliament, and the other one, William Huskisson, who was also present, said that there was no reason why the subscribers to the railway should be deterred, and whatever the temporary opposition, Parliament must ultimately give its sanction. Two resolutions, stated to have been drafted by Henry Booth, were passed in favour of the subscribers renewing their application in the next session.

Two decisive steps were taken by the Railway Committee in preparation for the renewed application. First, they negotiated with, and appointed on the 1st July 1825, Messrs. George and John Rennie, two of the best known civil engineers in the country, to make a new survey. The second, was to reduce the opposition of the canal companies. In 1824 they had approached, without success, Mr. R.H. Bradshaw MP, one of the Trustees* who managed the Duke of Bridgewater's Canal. In 1825 they approached the Marquis of Stafford, later the Duke of Sutherland, the beneficial owner of the canal. The outcome was that the Marquis of Stafford agreed to subscribe one thousand £100 shares. In return he was to appoint three of the fifteen directors of the new company. There was much rumour and gossip at the time as to how this was done, but Mr. James Loch MP, later a director of the railway, was certainly involved.**

The new prospectus was issued on the 26th December 1825 and once again was the work of Henry Booth. At the start it provided answers to the principal objections raised in and out of Parliament to the first Bill. First, to avoid any error in the survey, the Committee had '. . . engaged the professional services of most eminent Engineers, aided by assistants of undoubted talents and activity . . . .' Secondly, the new line was to reach the King's and Queen's Docks by a tunnel and

---

*One of the other Trustees was the Archbishop of York; Bishop of Carlisle when appointed, a brother-in-law of the Marquis of Stafford.

**In his *History of the Commerce and Town of Liverpool* Thomas Baines states that Charles Lawrence, John Moss and Robert Gladstone negotiated on their own responsibility, without informing the other members of the Committee, and that the suggestion came from Mr. Pritt, the Company's Solicitor, who got Mr. Adams, a relative of Mr. Loch, to open the negotiations.

inclined plane, avoiding any interference with the streets of
Liverpool. Thirdly, by stopping short at the Irwell at the
Manchester end, opposition from the old Quay Company
(Mersey & Irwell Canal Company) was reduced; the Canal
Company had claimed their navigation would be interfered
with by a bridge over the canal.* Fourthly, the Leeds &
Liverpool Canal Company had objected to the railway as it was
to have passed under their canal. 'However futile such an
objection, it is satisfactory to be enabled to state, that even this
assumed ground of opposition is altogether avoided, as the line
does not go near the canal in question.'

On the subject of locomotive engines, it had been claimed
that they were incompetent to do the tasks assigned to them,
were unsafe, and, in operation, a public nuisance. However,
Counsel for the opposition in Parliament, after the evidence
had been heard, had admitted that the first two claims were
incorrect. On the third, the Railway Committee were
confident that improved locomotives would be available which
would obviate all objections on the score of nuisance, but any
restriction Parliament might impose for the protection of
landowners or the public would be accepted. By changes in the
line of the railway, it was hoped that the opposition of the
Earls of Derby and Sefton and other landowners** would be
reduced. The rapid growth of trade between Liverpool and
Manchester demanded extra facilities, and this had induced
the Marquis of Stafford to subscribe to the railway.

After mentioning that the estimates of merchandise traffic
in the first prospectus had been admitted, when discussed in
the House of Commons Committee, to be too low, there
followed the remark:

'The travelling between Liverpool and Manchester is
upon the most extensive scale; and the economy to be
effected in this branch of expenditure, though impossible to

*In 1829, the railway obtained powers from Parliament to cross the Irwell, and
the bridge was completed shortly before the line was opened.
**One of these was Mrs. Earle, mother of Hardman Earle, later a Director of
the L&MR and L&NWR. In 1832 in the committee stage of the London &
Birmingham Bill in the House of Lords, he gave evidence of how groundless
their fears of the railway had proved to be.

be estimated with accuracy, must be considered as most important, and, of itself, no small recommendation of the undertaking.'

After some calculations on the amount of coal (one million tons per annum) that might be consumed in Liverpool and Manchester and a possible saving to the users of £100,000 per annum, the prospectus ended:

'But the subject does not end here. It becomes a question of serious import whether this country, which is indebted for so much of her wealth, and power, and greatness, to the bold and judicious application of mechanical science, shall now pause in the career of improvement, while it is notorious that other nations will adopt the means of aggrandisement which we reject — whether England shall relinquish the high vantage ground she at present possesses, not more with a reference to the direct operations of commerce and manufactures, than, generally, in the successful application of the most important principles of science and art.

'The Committee feels that it is unnecessary to dwell at greater length on the question they have thus brought before the public. They are about to apply for the sanction of the legislature; and they are determined to relax no efforts on their part to bring about the honourable and speedy accomplishment of the great work in which they have engaged.'

The following members of the Railway Committee were present in London when the new Bill was presented on the 7th February 1826 — Charles Lawrence, John Moss, Robert Gladstone, Joseph Sandars, Richard Harrison and Henry Booth. After an unopposed second reading on the 20th February, the committee stage opened on the 6th March. Opposition was mainly from certain landowners and the two remaining canal companies, while the Liverpool Corporation, in view of the changes in the line, no longer opposed it.

On the 16th March the Preamble was approved by 43 to 18 votes, and on the 6th April the third reading was carried by 88 votes to 41 against — majority 47. On the 7th April, General Gascoyne, who had presented the Bill on both occasions and been Chairman of the Commons Committee* dealing with it, delivered the Bill to the House of Lords. There was no opposition to the second reading in the Lords on the 10th April. The committee stage opened on the 13th April, and after some adjournments the Preamble was approved by 30 to 2 votes against. The Bill was read a third time and passed without a division, receiving the Royal Assent on the 5th May.

The members of the Railway Committee returned to Liverpool and the first meeting of the Liverpool & Manchester Railway proprietors took place on the 29th May 1826. Charles Lawrence having been called to the chair, he reported that the costs of the two applications for the Bill had been £33,000 in two almost equal amounts of £16,000. The first item on the agenda was to choose the two officials of the company appointed by the proprietors, the Treasurer and the Clerk. There was a recommendation from the committee that the Treasurer's salary should be £500 per annum. Mr. John Gladstone MP, a member of the 1822 Committee, who had sold his shares in the company to his son Robert, so as to be free to give unfettered support to the Bills in Parliament, moved an amendment, which was lost, that this be increased to £600. Henry Booth was unanimously appointed Treasurer and Mr. Pritt of the Company's solicitors, Pritt & Clay, was appointed Clerk, to be remunerated by the fees he would earn.

There was then some discussion on the propriety of remunerating the Directors for their services, and it was eventually agreed that this should be 1 guinea per meeting, not more than fifty-two meetings in the year to be paid for, and that to receive this sum the Directors must not be more than five minutes late for the meeting and not leave until the end.

There then took place a ballot for the Directors and the following were elected:

Robert Benson, James Bourne, Dr. T.S. Brandreth, Lister Ellis, Robert Gladstone, Richard Harrison, Adam Hodgson, Charles Lawrence, John Moss, William Rathbone,

*Up to 1846 local MPs were always put on the committees dealing with Railway Bills. Mr. W.E. Gladstone prohibited the continuance of this practice in the Railway Bill of that year.

William Rotheram, Joseph Sandars.

The Marquis of Stafford appointed the following Directors: Captain J. Bradshaw, Mr. J. Loch MP, and Mr. J. Sothern.

The report to the 1826 meeting ended with the statement that the Committee looked forward to the locomotive engine as the power advantageous to the company and the public. 'They have never doubted that the ingenuity of the country would be exerted to construct an efficient and unobjectionable machine for this purpose.'

When in March 1831 it was realized that the railway was going to be successful, a number of resolutions of thanks were passed at a general meeting on the 18th May. The warmest thanks of the proprietors went '. . . to our Treasurer, Mr. Booth, not only for his conduct of his own particular department, but for his able and effectual assistance in improving the power of the locomotive engine.'

In 1834 the proprietors wished to express their appreciation in a more tangible form, and it was proposed to present the five members* of the Railway Committee and Henry Booth with 100 guineas and a piece of plate suitably inscribed.**

*Charles Lawrence, John Moss and Joseph Sandars did not accept the gifts.
**Inscription on silver tray presented to Henry Booth:
PRESENTED
to
HENRY BOOTH ESQUIRE
By the
PROPRIETORS Of The LIVERPOOL & MANCHESTER RAILWAY,
In Testimony of his valuable Services
as Honorary Secretary to the General Committee,
In The Memorable Proceedings Before Parliament,
in the Years 1825 and 1826;
during which period he devoted himself to the arduous duties of his situation,
With Zeal, Regularity and Perseverance;
and uniting with these qualities extensive scientific attainments,
essentially contributed to promote the ultimate objects of an undertaking,
For Magnificence of Design and
Utility Of Purpose, Preeminent,
amongst the Works of modern times.

Chapter IV

The Liverpool & Manchester Railway Board held its first meeting on Tuesday, the 30th May 1826, and resolved to meet in future at noon every Monday,* the meetings to last two hours. Henry Booth acted as Secretary and the first minutes are in his handwriting; subsequently he made notes at the meetings and these were later copied into the minute book by a clerk.**

At the next few meetings the principal business w⌣ the appointment of an engineer, and the acquisition of land and property. A committee of Directors was appointed to purchase land and Mr. Lister Ellis was empowered to treat for the lease for three years of a house in Clayton Square. This became for many years the offices of the company, a room being set aside for the board room.

The appointment of the Engineer took several meetings. The Rennies were approached, but their terms were unacceptable. Finally, on the 3rd July, the Board resolved

---

*The meeting for Monday, the 12th June was held on Friday, the 9th June owing to the General Election on the Monday. This was an unusually quiet election for Liverpool, lasting barely a day. Of the six candidates, Mr. Huskisson and General Gascoyne gained 113 and 103 votes respectively. Two of the other four candidates obtained 26 and 13 votes and of the remaining two, each received 3 votes.

**In the Minute Book of the Grand Junction Railway, where Henry Booth acted as Secretary to the local Board, after the formation of the L&NWR, drafts for the minutes of their monthly meetings from the 12th June 1850 to the 11th February 1851 are preserved.

unanimously to offer the position to George Stephenson. Those who favoured him, among whom was the Treasurer, made sure that the Board was fully acquainted with his capabilities and suitability for the post. Mr. Sandars had been to inspect the railways in the North-East for which George Stephenson had been responsible, and he had obtained the views of the people he had spoken to there as to his ability. Dr. Brandreth had made enquiries as to the terms which would be acceptable — £800 per annum, including all travelling, and to work nine months in the year; there were testimonials from Edward Pease, Chairman of the Stockton & Darlington Railway and Mr. Longridge of the Bedlington Iron Works. It was also resolved to appoint as Consulting Engineer, Mr. J. Jessop, with whom the Rennies had been prepared to work. He died in October 1826, and George Stephenson became sole Engineer, apart from the few occasions when a further opinion was needed on some specialized matter.

At the end of July the Board turned its attention to the position of the Treasurer. The Liverpool & Manchester Railway Act required the Company '. . . to take sufficient security from every person who shall hereafter be appointed treasurer of the said Company, and from the receiver, collector or other officer having the custody or control of any money received by virtue of this Act, for the faithful execution of his office, before he shall enter thereupon.'

The Finance Committee — Robert Benson, William Rathbone and William Rotheram — was instructed to find proper security from the Treasurer and it was reported on the 7th August that he had not at present any funds at the disposal of the Directors. However, on the 1st September, the committee's minutes recorded that a bond had been received from Henry Booth in £5,000, and approved. Where he obtained the sum required is obscure. Thomas Booth, in his Will made in 1824, listed sums advanced to his three eldest sons, to be deducted from their share of his estate on his death. As Henry Booth had received £4,500, it seems probable that his father had also assisted him in this matter.

During the next few years the Treasurer's duties were not onerous; with frequent meetings of the Board or of committees, his secretarial duties were greater. However,

Henry Booth had time to consider the problems of the motive power for the railway, and these are dealt with in the next chapter. He also took a prominent part in a wide range of activities in the town: the amendment of the Corn Laws, the monopoly of the East India Company in trade with the Far East, the repeal of the Corporation and Test Acts, and Parliamentary Reform. He also became a member of the Anti-Slavery Society.*

On Wednesday, the 15th November 1826, there was a meeting at the Town Hall, with the Mayor in the chair, on the subject of the Corn Laws. From 1793 until 1815 the importation of corn and other cereals had been permitted on payment of the appropriate duty, which varied with the price of corn in England. The amount imported was usually approximately 600,000 quarters, about two weeks' consumption. In 1821, elaborate rules had been fixed for calculating the average price of corn, based on the figures realized each week in the principal market towns, the average figure being published in the London Gazette. In 1822 an Act was passed to prohibit the importation of corn unless the domestic price was above 70/- per quarter, and a sliding scale of duties, based on the home price, was imposed on any corn imported or released from bonded warehouses. In 1825 and 1826 similar Acts had to be passed to provide supplies before the harvest. In 1826 a further Act was passed to permit the importation of up to 500,000 quarters of wheat by Order in Council before the end of that year. The duty to be paid was to be fixed by the Order, but was not to exceed the 1822 rate.

There was an account of the meeting in the *Liverpool Mercury* on the 17th November. In the absence of Sir John Tobin,** the first resolution was moved by Henry Booth. He pointed out that the Corn Laws caused privation and misery to the great mass of the population. Communities of people had been content to suffer for a long while before stirring themselves to procure the redress of public grievances. He

---

*The leader of this movement in Liverpool was James Cropper, a member of the first Liverpool & Manchester Railway Committee, who had replaced Dr. Brandreth on the L&MR Board in 1827.
**Mayor 1819-20, a member of the Liverpool & Manchester Railway Committee.

could not otherwise account for the apathy with respect to the monopoly of that most important article — human food. According to the Parliamentary Committee, good land in Great Britain produced 34 to 40 bushels of corn per acre, the worst 8 to 10 bushels. The price of corn was regulated by the cost of cultivation, in some cases four times what it should have been. Taking good and bad together, the cost was double that of the great corn producers in Europe. The most moderate duty proposed — 10/- a quarter — continued to keep corn prices much higher than they should be. Land owners argued that they required high prices because of the high taxation needed to pay interest on the National Debt. In point of fact, the consumer paid the tax and it would be better if he did it directly and paid less for food.

He was glad that the workers on the soil were beginning to see that they were not benefiting from the present system and that their interests were inseparable from those of other workers. In view of the present distresses of manufacturers, it was becoming more apparent that the loss sustained by lack of demand more than balanced the apparent advantages of the Corn Laws. The question, therefore, must be whether we should consume foreign corn or none, and the price of wheat was not the main consideration; it was that there should be an equivalent market for the consumption of the produce of labour in manufacturing. It was the subject of deepest importance and he rejoiced that a proper feeling respecting it had gone abroad. Such a satire upon legislation as the Corn Laws could not long be suffered to disgrace the Statute Book amongst an enlightened community. The present administration was generally friendly to the principle of Free Trade and he hoped it was particularly so with regard to corn. He called on the people of Liverpool to declare unequivocally their approbation of these principles. They owed it to themselves to show their representative [Huskisson] that they were not insensible to the benefits of that liberal system of commercial policy, which had struggled into existence during his administration.*

*As President of the Board of Trade.

After Mr. Nicholas Robinson* had seconded the resolution, the next one was proposed by Mr. W.W. Currie** and he commenced his speech by saying that he would not dwell on the powerful reasons in favour of change; they had been most ably stated by Mr. Booth.

Henry Booth was next concerned with the movement to get the Corporation and Test Acts repealed. Under these Acts, passed in the reign of Charles II, to hold office or be employed by municipal corporations, it was necessary to take Holy Communion according to the Rites of the Church of England, Church of Ireland or the Presbyterian Church of Scotland, depending on where the office was to be taken up. A similar test was also applied to employment under the Crown.

In 1787 and 1788 attempts had been made to repeal the Acts and in the Commons on the second attempt the motion was lost by only twenty votes (124 to 104). In consequence of the French Revolution in 1789, the next attempt in 1790 was decisively defeated by 189 votes (294 to 105). At the end of 1826, Mr. John Smith MP, brother of Lord Carrington, gave notice that he intended to move the repeal of the Test Act, when the annual Indemnity Bill came up. At the end of March or early April at this period, an Act was regularly passed to indemnify those who had inadvertently infringed the Acts.

In Liverpool, Thomas Fletcher heard of the move from his brother-in-law Henry Enfield, who was a friend of Mr. Smith. As a result, a meeting of representatives of all denominations of Dissenters was held at the George Inn, with the Rev. William Shepherd in the chair. It was not well attended and Thomas Fletcher decided to prepare a petition independently. This he did with the aid of a forty-year-old pamphlet on the subject, by a Mr. Sergeant Heywood. His petition was signed by a large number of Liverpool Presbyterians and he sent it to Mr. Huskisson on the 5th April 1827. At the same time Thomas Fletcher wrote to Mr. Smith and he replied: 'If you

---

*Nicholas Robinson was later a Director of the L&MR. He was Mayor in 1828-29. In the Mayoral Election in 1827 he was the unsuccessful candidate. The contest lasted six days, the votes always being equal, costing at the finish £20 to £30 a vote.

**First Mayor in the Reformed Council in 1836. Later Director of the L&MR, nominated by the Marquis of Stafford. Died on the 4th November 1840.

are correct that I have been instrumental in any degree in bringing before Parliament the consideration of the Corporation and Test Acts, it will ever be to me a most pleasing reflection; for I am decidedly of opinion that the Dissenters by their apathy or want of judgement have permitted a system to be hitherto perpetuated which cannot stand the effects of discussion.'

Nothing was actually achieved in this year because of the instability of the Government, but in 1828 Dissenters throughout the country took more positive action. According to the *Liverpool Mercury*, 1,700 petitions were presented to Parliament. Among those who decided to send a petition was the congregation of Renshaw Street Chapel. In view of his experience in such matters Henry Booth, with two others, was asked to draft the petition. It was approved by the congregation on the 3rd February and details appeared in the *Liverpool Mercury* on the 8th February. Mr. William Roscoe, MP for Liverpool in 1806, was a member of the congregation, and the point was made that a Dissenter could be a Member of Parliament, but not an excise man, the humblest position in the employment of the Crown. In view of the large contribution Dissenters had made to their country in science, literature and the arts, and by their industry, skill and enterprise to its wealth, power and resources, the continuous existence of the Acts was both anomalous and oppressive. The petition was presented to the House of Lords by the Marquis of Lansdowne and the Earl of Derby, and in the Commons by Mr. Huskisson and General Gascoyne.

The repeal of the Acts was moved by Lord John Russell and seconded by Mr. John Smith on the 26th February 1828, and carried by a majority of 44, and received the Royal Assent on the 9th May. To hold office it was then only necessary to swear that one was not against the Church of England and Protestantism.

On the 19th June, in Liverpool, to celebrate the repeal, a public dinner attended by 160 guests was held at the King's Arms. The Rev. Shepherd was in the chair, and after he had spoken, Mr. Ryley sang an appropriate song. Then, according to the *Liverpool Mercury*, Henry Booth addressed the company at considerable length. He contrasted the character of the noble marquis, the Marquis of Lansdowne, with the intolerance of the Duke of Newcastle and other peers, reading extracts from their speeches in the debates on the repeal. The repeal was one step towards the complete extension of civil and religious freedom to all classes. Among others, there were speeches by Thomas Fletcher and William Rathbone and from Mr. Ryley there was another song.

The *Liverpool Mercury*, which was published the next day, apologized that owing to the lateness of the hour, only an outline of the speeches could be given.

For years shipowners and merchants had been complaining about the monopoly of the East India Company in trade with India and the Far East and the West Indian Merchants had the added burden of having to pay an extra duty on sugar. On the 28th January 1829, Mr. Nicholas Robinson, the Mayor, called a public meeting on the subject in the Court Room. The second resolution was moved by James Cropper, and Henry Booth, who had been taking an active part in the campaign, seconded the resolution, and according to the *Liverpool Mercury*, spoke to the following effect:

'I feel called upon, Mr. Mayor, thus publicly to enter my protest against a system so full of evil as that which has long prevailed under the East India Company. When the true character of this odious monopoly is understood, the speedy extinction of the system and its injurious consequences must follow.

'The Company consists of 5,000 individuals, only a small proportion of the 23 million of this kingdom and of the thousand million of British subjects spread over the plains of Hindustan. You will be surprised to hear that of the 5,000 individuals, 4,950 have no more to do with the management or partake of profits of the concern than any individuals of this assembly. (Hear Hear and applause) Of the small remnant, the Directors and their immediate friends and dependents have the management and enjoy the profits of the monopoly and on them and their heads, therefore, the responsibility for mismanagement ought to rest.

'When we consider the richness of the soils of India and China, well suited to the culture of almost every article which the earth produces, it is scarcely possible to be too sanguine on the contemplation of the benefits which will proceed from an unrestricted intercourse with these countries.

'I finally hope that England famed as she is for the multiplicity of her charitable institutions and her promptness to support any scheme for the well-being of mankind, will not be backward on the present occasion or neglect this opportunity of doing so much good to so many people. The most prominent facts with regard to the removal of restrictions to our intercourse with the East, that we shall have a more abundant supply of their produce at a cheaper rate, and in return dispose of a far greater quantity of our own manufactures. The advantages of these measures will be unfolded by the gentlemen who follow me, but one of them I will again mention, employment of our industrious and deserving population. My object in our intercourse with the East is not that the rich should have an accession of wealth, as that the poor should have more bread. (Great applause)'

In the autumn of 1828 the problem of motive power for the L&MR was still unsettled. It was reported that the Stockton & Darlington Railway was having difficulties with its locomotives. The Board decided to send a further deputation to the North-East, and arrangements were made for Henry Booth to accompany James Cropper to Darlington, where they were to meet John Moss, the third member of the delegation. James Cropper, who wrote the report was against locomotives and, as a result, it came out in favour of using rope haulage with stationary engines. The report was printed and George Stephenson was asked to comment on it, which he did on the 5th November. Reading Stephenson's comments today, it seems clear that he demolished the case for fixed engines. The Board, however, was not satisfied and engaged two eminent Engineers, Mr. John Rastrick of Stourbridge and Mr. James Walker of London, to look further into the matter. They also reported in favour of fixed engines, but showed that the capital cost of these would be higher than for locomotive engines, but that the running costs would be less. In

consequence, there was a good argument for the use of
locomotives, in that less capital would be needed until there
was some clear knowledge of the probable traffic. As a result,
on the 20th April, the important decision was reached to offer
a prize of £500 for the best improved locomotive.* The
consequences of this proposal are dealt with in the following
chapter.

In addition to presenting accounts at the end of each half
year, Henry Booth wrote the Directors' reports to the
Shareholders on these occasions. The Directors usually made
some slight amendments, but essentially they represented the
views of Henry Booth.

In a period of high unemployment, the Government was
prepared, as is the case today, to make loans to companies
which had schemes to provide work, and in its second Act, the
L&MR obtained powers to borrow money from the Treasury
Commissioners. To check that the works, for which the money
had been advanced, were being properly executed, the
Government sent Mr. Thomas Telford, the well-known
engineer, to inspect the line at the end of November 1828.
There were some scathing remarks about Mr. Telford's report
to the Commissioners, in the report to the Shareholders on the
18th March 1829. '. . . a document than which one more
abounding with inaccuracies and erroneous statements can
hardly be conceived; and all the errors being on the
unfavourable side, the impression conveyed to the Commissioners was that a large sum of money, beyond the
resources of the Company, would be required to finish the
Railway, and that the period of the completion was distant
and uncertain. . . .' However, a deputation of Directors went
to London and succeeded in convincing the Commissioners of
the inaccuracy of these statements.

The report to the Shareholders on the 10th August 1829
ended:

'In conclusion, the Directors congratulate the proprietors
on the near approach to the completion of the great work in
which they are engaged; and they need hardly repeat their

---

*The Stipulations and Conditions are in Appendix I.

entire confidence in the correctness of that view of the whole scheme which induced them originally to consider it not only as highly interesting and important to the kingdom at large, and to this town in particular, but as affording a safe and very lucrative investment of capital to the Shareholders in the undertaking.'

There can be little doubt that the views expressed in these two extracts are those of Henry Booth.

Mr James Foster, the Manager at the Earl of Dudley's colliery near Stourbridge, which operated the Shut End Railway, which opened on the 2nd June 1829 conveying coal from the colliery to a neighbouring canal, had repeatedly asked for a visit of inspection to this railway. The engine in use, the Agenoria, had been designed by John Rastrick and, according to the *Birmingham Gazette*, on the opening day had hauled twenty wagons carrying 920 passengers and 42 tons of coal, a total load of 131½ tons, for one mile at 11 miles an hour, the line falling on a gradient of 1 - 330. At the beginning of September 1829, one of the L&MR's Directors, Mr. Charles Tayleur,* with George Stephenson and Henry Booth, visited the line, and on the 7th September Mr. Tayleur reported to the Board on this visit. It was mentioned that the engine ran with little puffing; puffing being one of the objections to steam locomotives. He also reported that a glass tube was provided to show the height of the water in the boiler, which Mr. Tayleur considered very desirable, and that there was little smoke and the engine moved easily and smoothly.

*In 1832 Charles Tayleur in partnership with Robert Stephenson founded a locomotive factory at Newton-le-Willows. The firm later took the name of Vulcan Foundry.

The Agenoria

Chapter V

THE ROCKET AND RAINHILL

Two problems had to be solved if the railway was to be worked by locomotives. The 1826 Liverpool and Manchester Act specified that locomotives should consume their own smoke. This meant that coke, rather than coal, would have to be burnt. The other problem was that none of the boilers on the locomotives in use produced, in the limited space available, enough steam to drive trains at more than 8 to 10 miles an hour. While this was adequate for the carriage of goods, it would not be enough for passenger traffic to compete with 8 miles an hour achieved by horse drawn coaches, and was the reason why there was only vague mention of passenger business in the prospectuses; in fact, after the opening of the line, passenger revenue was always greater than that for goods traffic.

The problem of how to produce more steam had been in the minds of engineers for over fifty years.

The patent most mentioned in this connection is that of Mr. James Neville* in which the heat goes to the top of a vertical boiler in thirty-two 2½″ diameter copper tubes and then descends to the bottom in three larger tubes to reach the chimney from the bottom of the boiler. Looking at this patent specification and the drawings attached to it, no one would get any useful ideas for the construction of a locomotive boiler.

Other patents all obtained extra heating surface by having

---

*Patent No. 5344, 14/3/1826.

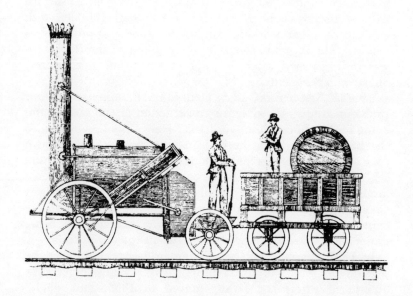

The Rocket

tubes containing water heated by the fire. In one patent* Mr. Alexander Clarke specifies copper water tubes and the use of distilled water, essential for this type of boiler.

The whole problem had actually been fully dealt with in a patent of November 1788 in which Mr. James Rumsey, a versatile engineer, described many methods of providing extra heating surface employing heated air, flame or 'smoak' to warm the water. In one of the boilers, the 'smoak' goes through vertical tubes inside the boilers to the chimney. For anyone with time to study patent specifications, there was a multiplicity of methods for providing a greater heating surface with stationary boilers, but for a locomotive boiler with entirely different working conditions, a new approach was needed. The ultimate solution — the boiler of the Rocket — was only reached after two unsuccessful, but not entirely abortive experiments.

George Stephenson and Henry Booth discussed these problems frequently while the construction of the railway was going on.** On the 30th April 1827 Henry Booth reported to the L&MR Board that he had an idea on how best to burn coke in a locomotive boiler without smoke. George Stephenson said that if an experiment based on the idea was successful on a large scale, it would be highly important to the Railway Company. The Board authorized him to make the requisite experiments to test the merits of the scheme, it being understood that £100 would be sufficient for the purpose.

In 1827 Henry Booth was living in Lodge Lane and he presumably had similar facilities there as in Abercromby Square to where the family moved in 1833, and where, according to Mary Anne Booth he had a room devoted to scientific and mechanical experiments, and planned and matured his inventions.

On the 7th January 1828 George Stephenson read a report to the Board on the subject of a locomotive engine and boiler on a new construction — the result of the experiment which he and the Treasurer had been authorized to carry out. The Board was shown drawings of the locomotive engine and boiler

---

*Patent No. 4665, 1822.
**J.C. Jeaffreson *Life of Robert Stephenson* Vol. I, p. 119.

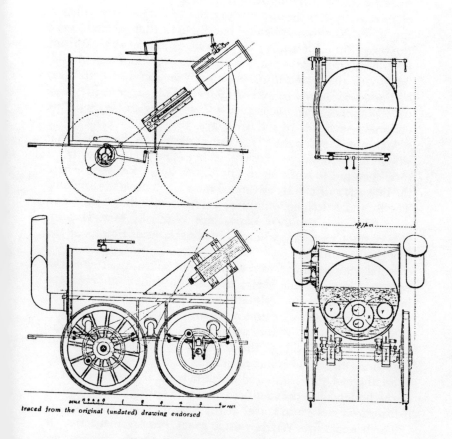

traced from the original (undated) drawing endorsed

The Lancashire Witch — original design

and it was resolved that the Engineer* should construct an engine on this plan, weight not to exceed 6 tons and to be able to draw 20 tons of goods or sixty passengers; the cost to be £550.

In the records of Robert Stephenson & Company there is a drawing of the original design, but the actual boiler was less elaborate, having the two fire places inside two large tubes in the boiler. Robert Stephenson had thought that he could bend the boiler tubes, but this proved to be impracticable. Writing to Robert on the 31st January 1828, George Stephenson said: 'Mr Booth and myself think two chimneys would be better, say 8″ diameter and not to exceed 15 feet.' This suggests the large tube branched into two return tubes ending in two separate chimneys each side of the fire place.

Mr. John Moss on the 21st April suggested to the Board that when the locomotive arrived, it being expected shortly, it should be put to work on the Bolton & Leigh Railway, where the line was sufficiently advanced for a locomotive to run on it. The Bolton & Leigh Committee agreed to use the engine, and on arrival it was named Lancashire Witch by Mrs. Hulton, wife of the Chairman, who placed a garland of flowers at the foot of the funnel.

Robert Stephenson had returned from South America at the end of 1827 and while Henry Booth was producing new ideas in boiler construction, Robert had plans for improving the efficiency of the engine and reducing its size and ugliness.

The Lancashire Witch was carried on springs, and the cylinders, on each side of the boiler at the fire box end, drove the wheels direct. This was possible because the cylinders were at an angle of 39°, compared with the vertical cylinders on top of the boilers used previously. The use of springs was essential if locomotives were to travel at the higher speeds envisaged.

The Lancashire Witch was a great improvement on all previous locomotives. Rastrick and Walker's report on Locomotives and Fixed Engines would have been more favourable to the locomotive, if they had seen the engine

*As shown in the Minutes, this order and the one for an engine in March 1829 were given to the Engineer and executed by Robert Stephenson & Company. George Stephenson was a partner in the firm, started in 1823, and the management of it was not taken over by Robert until 1827.

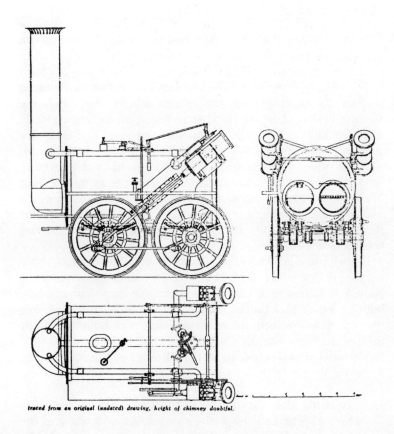

traced from an original (undated) drawing, height of chimney doubtful.

The Lancashire Witch — as built

E

working. They only had figures of its performance given to them by George Stephenson and Mr. Sinclair, Clerk to the Bolton & Leigh Railway. Mr. Rastrick did not believe that the engine could have done the work — hauling 58 tons up an incline of 1 in 432 at 8 miles an hour, which he calculated to be 21.6 hp — unless the safety valve had been tied down to obtain a higher pressure than 50 lbs per square inch.

It was intended that the Lancashire Witch should burn coke, and the draught for the fire was created by two bellows worked by excentrics on the tender wheels, but with the simpler design of boiler these were found to be unnecessary, and were later removed. Experiments continued and there is a note in Henry Booth's writing at the end of the L&MR Board Minutes of the 1st December 1828: 'Reported at this meeting that Mr. Benson, Mr. Cropper, Mr. Bourne went on the 26th November to inspect a coke boiler on *a new construction* which Mr. Robert Stephenson got made at Wallasey, & which raised steam abundantly, without smoke — The Experiment appears satisfactory — HB.'

Describing the same experiment, Robert Stephenson wrote on the 1st December to Mr. Longridge, one of the partners in Robert Stephenson & Company that: 'We have had my new boiler tried at Mr. Laird's Manufactory. Built to burn coke, the experiment was completely successful.' The boiler was then shipped to Newcastle by Carlisle.

The next step is recorded in the Minutes of the meeting on the 16th March 1829:

'It being thought desirable to work part of the Line between Marle Cutting at the west of Olive Mount and the Broad Green Embankment with a Locomotive engine, Mr. Stephenson was directed to provide an engine for the purpose which he stated he could have ready in 6 or 8 weeks.'

This locomotive was built by Robert Stephenson & Company, and had two similar boilers, one of which was the one tested at Laird's. It had six coupled wheels, and the cylinders were at an angle and in similar positions to those on the Lancashire Witch. During manufacture it was known as

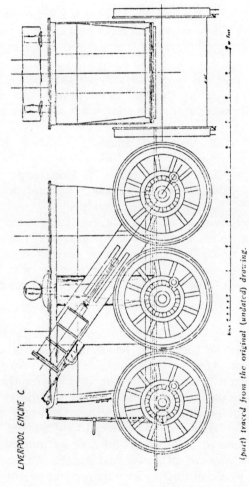

LIVERPOOL ENGINE 6

(part) traced from the original (undated) drawing.

The Twin Sisters

the Liverpool Coke Engine, but as the Twin Sisters on the L&MR. Writing to Timothy Hackworth, Locomotive Superintendant of the Stockton & Darlington Railway on the 30th April, Robert Stephenson & Company said:

'Our Liverpool Locomotive Engine has been tried and works beautifully — we expect Mr. George Stephenson will be here to see her before she leaves the manufactory.'

The engine reached Liverpool only on the 13th July and proved satisfactory, doing the work of ten horses at less cost; it continued to be used on construction work after the railway was opened.

In August 1829 George Stephenson summed up the performance of these two engines in a letter to the chief draughtsman at Robert Stephenson & Company's Works saying that: '. . . the coke engine is doing extremely well, but the Lancashire Witch is rely doing wonders.'

After the Twin Sisters had been ordered, Henry Booth had a new idea for a boiler, and when it was suggested that there should be a prize for the best improved locomotive, his first action was to discuss this with George Stephenson with a view to building an engine with a boiler of the new design and enter it for the competition. To quote his own words:*

'When the line was so far constructed that a distance of two miles, on the summit of Rainhill, on nearly a level plain, was completed — that is to say on the 20th April 1829 — the Directors offered a premium of £500 for the most efficient locomotive engine on certain conditions prescribed, one of which was that the weight was not to exceed six tons — and "that less weight would be preferred". This condition I refer to, as showing how little we understood at that date the measure of power and consequent weight of engine that would ultimately be required to give scope and effect to the railway locomotive, considering the work it would have to do — the weight in fact was increased from year to year till at length it has reached some twenty-six

Alfred Booth p. 20-22.

tons, and sometimes heavier, instead of six as then arbitrarily prescribed.

'The power of a steam-engine at that time as well as now depended on the rapidity with which steam could be produced, and the limited weight allowed by the conditions very much increased the difficulty. The problem to be solved was by what contrivance the largest quantity of steam could be raised in the shortest time, and in the smallest compass. In considering this question, it struck me that a great point would be gained, if by some contrivance we could bring the fire into closer proximity to the water to be boiled, and at the same time expose a larger heated surface to the water. I thought that this might be done. If, instead of passing the fire through the boiler by means of one large iron tube twelve inches diameter constructed of iron nearly half an inch thick, we could carry the fire through a multitude of copper tubes only two or three inches diameter and about the sixteenth of an inch thick, the point would be gained. We should obtain a much increased surface of heated metal exposed to the fire, while the fire at the same time would be brought much closer to the water, and the caloric therefore be so much the more readily introduced into the water, and steam consequently be so much more rapidly generated, which was the object to be accomplished.

'I mentioned my scheme to Mr. Stephenson, and asked him if he would join me in building a locomotive to compete for the prize of £500 offered by the Directors, subject of course to the conditions prescribed. Mr. Stephenson took a day or two to look into the merits of the plan I proposed, and then told me he thought it would do, and would join me in the venture. It was agreed that Mr. Robert Stephenson, who was an engine builder at Newcastle-on-Tyne, should construct the competing locomotive, and was set to work accordingly. The important day of the competition was the 8th October 1829,* but some time previous to that date Mr. Stephenson told me that his son Robert (who was building

---

*The trial of the Rocket was on the 8th October. The competition was to have started on the 1st October, but the opening was postponed until the 6th October to allow the competitors more time for preparation.

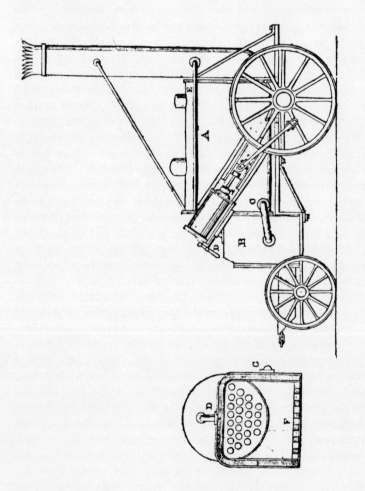

The Rocket

the engine at Newcastle) was very desirous to become a partner with his father and me in the venture for the prize. I had no wish to dilute my interest in the little speculation I had entered upon, but as father and son seemed bent on it, I made no objection, and it was settled that we should share the profit or loss in the speculation proportionally, that is in thirds.'

However, there were serious problems in the manufacture of the boiler. These are described in letters from Robert Stephenson to Henry Booth. The letters were exhibited at the Franco-British Exhibition in London in 1908 and are quoted in full by W.L. Steel.* The originals were destroyed by fire, but facsimile copies are in the Public Record Office. The conditions of the competition necessitated the boiler being given an hydraulic test to 150 lbs per square inch. This presented considerable difficulties. With the advice of George Stephenson the difficulties were overcome, but only in time to have the locomotive, which was named the Rocket, given a short trial run on the Killingworth Railway. The engine was then sent by road to Carlisle and shipped by steamer to Liverpool, and the Board was informed of its arrival on the 28th September.

Meanwhile on the 31st August the Board had ordered:

'. . . that the place of the Tryal for the Specimen Engines on the 1st October next, be the level space between the two Inclined Planes at Rainhill; and that the Engineer prepare a double Railway for the two miles of level, and a single line from Rainhill down the plane to the Roby Embankment.

'Resolved that Mr. Rastrick and Mr. Nicholas Wood be written to, to request their attendance professionally on the first and second week in October . . . and report to the Directors.'

Mr Hodgson was requested to write to Mr. John Kennedy, to ask him to join the two Engineers and act with them as Judges

---

*The History of the London and North Western Railway. Copies of the letters are in Appendix II.

of the competition.

Six newspapers in Liverpool reported the competition in detail and it was attended by Mr. Robertson, editor of the *Mechanic's Magazine*, who wrote a detailed account for the magazine. In addition, Robert Stephenson and Joseph Locke, in their book *Observations of the comparative Merits of Locomotives and Fixed Engines*, published in February 1830, appended an account of the competition.

Of the six Liverpool newspapers, *The Albion* appeared on Monday, the *Liverpool Courier* and the *Liverpool Times* on Wednesday, the *Liverpool Mercury* was published on Friday and the *Liverpool Chronicle* and *Gores General Advertiser* on Saturday.

The accounts in the *Liverpool Mercury* and the *Mechanic's Magazine* have been used as the principal sources in most books on the subject, but a true picture of the contest can only be obtained by reading all the papers on the subject; for instance, *The Albion* is the only one to give an account of the Engineers' Dinner held on the 10th October.*

On the 5th October at a meeting of the L&MR Board the Engineer reported that '. . . the arrangements for trying the Specimen Engines were made and that they would be ready to start from Rainhill Bridge at 11 o'clock on the morrow.' It was ordered:

'That 300 men be provided with Staffs to act as Constables, for the preservation of good order, and that no person shall be admitted on the Railway . . . without a Ticket from the Directors, and that the Railway Carriage for the accommodation of the Directors be ready to start from the crossing of the Huyton Turnpike Road, at 10 o'clock in the morning.'

What was not mentioned was that Henry Booth and Robert Stephenson knew from tests which they had made on the Rocket that it would be able to take the Directors' carriage up the incline from Huyton to Rainhill.

---

*The Albion account implies that the dinner was held on Tuesday the 6th October, but a note in the *Liverpool Mercury* on the 16th mentioned the dinner as being on Saturday the 10th October.

Reporting on the start of the Trials, *Gores General Advertiser* said:

'The directors, each of whom wore a distinctive badge, arrived shortly after 10 a.m. from Huyton in cars drawn by Mr. Stephenson's locomotive steam carriage which moved up the inclined plane from thence with great velocity. They were accompanied by many scientific gentlemen whose presence was hailed with numerous cheers.'

It was a fine day and:

'. . . the ground at Rainhill exhibited a very lively appearance. A commodious tent had been erected for the accommodation of ladies and to serve as a grandstand. The sides of the race ground were lined with carriages of all descriptions; in short, the tout ensemble exhibited as much bustle and excitement as if the great St. Leger had been about to be contested.'*

The crowd was estimated at between 10,000 and 15,000. The *Liverpool Mercury* reported that the accommodation for refreshments and more solid comfort was lamentably deficient. Another tent provided bread and cheese and beer, but nothing better, and the wants of very few could be attended to in the two adjacent crowded public houses. However, the *Liverpool Courier* said that at the Railway Tavern there was a room set aside for better class visitors, who appeared pleased with the accommodation provided.

During the forenoon the locomotive carriages ran up and down the road for the amusement of the visitors, '. . . surprising and even startling the unscientific beholders by the amazing velocity by which they moved along the rails'.** 'A simultaneous burst of applause followed the appearance of the different carriages and their first movements were observed with the most breathless attention.'***

Stephenson & Locke pp. 64-65.
**The Albion.*
***Gores General Advertiser.*

The Cycloped

The competitors were:

1. Messrs. Braithwaite and Ericsson of London — 'The Novelty', Copper and Blue, weight 2 tons 15 cwt.
2. Mr. Hackworth of Darlington — 'The Sans Pareil', Green, Yellow and Black, weight 4 tons 8 cwt 2 qrs.
3. Mr. Robert Stephenson of Newcastle-upon-Tyne — the 'Rocket', Yellow and Black, White Chimney, weight 4 tons 3 cwt.
4. Mr. Brandreth of Liverpool — 'The Cycloped', worked by Horses, weight 3 tons.
5. Mr. Burstall of Edinburgh — 'The Perseverance', Red Wheels, weight 2 tons 17 cwt.

Unfortunately, the Perseverance had been dropped when being loaded on to a wagon at the Liverpool Docks and it was still undergoing repairs at the start of the contest.

Mr. Ross Winans' machine worked by two men was also on exhibition. Its speed could not be compared with that of the locomotives, but it went quite fast until one of its wheels was slightly damaged by Mr. Hackworth's locomotive.

'Mr. Robert Stephenson's carriage particularly attracted the attention of beholders. It ran without any weight 26 miles per hour shooting past the spectators with arrow swiftness, emitting very little smoke, but dropping red hot cinders. Cars containing stones were then attached to it to a gross weight of 17-tons and it was supposed that the contest would then commence, but the remainder of the day was consumed in the exhibition of the respective powers of the different machines, the Rocket with a load of 12½-tons running at 15 to 16 miles per hour.'*

It was the Novelty, however, which got the most attention, both on the opening day and all through the contest. The *Liverpool Courier* said, 'It seemed indeed to fly, presenting one of the most sublime spectacles of human ingenuity and human daring the world ever beheld. It actually made one giddy to look at it, it was a most sublime sight.' *The Albion* described its appearance and compactness as the beau idéal of

Gores General Advertiser.

The Novelty

a locomotive.

During the day a meeting of the engineers:

'. . . took place on the race ground. It was adjourned to the Waterloo, where a series of resolutions were passed which showed the spirit which actuated the meeting. In consequence of these resolutions the committee of engineers invited the whole of the Directors and officers of the Railway Company, and also Dr. Traill, the President of the Liverpool Royal Institution [to dinner at the Waterloo].* The Chair was taken by Mr. Rastrick, supported by Mr. Wood and Mr. Hartley as Vice-Chairmen, at each end of the table, the Stewards being judiciously interspersed among the company. The arrangements were made by the committee after the manner of the public dinners in London on great occasions, and appeared to cause some little surprise to those Liverpool gentlemen who had not before seen this mode of marshalling the company.

'Of the dinner . . . it is sufficient to observe that it was prepared by Mr. Lynn, whose excellent judgement in wines precludes the necessity of saying that they excelled. A part of the Harmonic Band were in attendance, and contributed to enliven the evening by playing several choice airs.

'On the cloth being drawn, the health of "The King" was given from the Chair. . . . The next toast was "The Liverpool and Manchester Rail-way, with our best wishes for its success." This toast was drunk with thrice three most enthusiastic cheers. Tune, "Off she goes".'

Over thirty toasts were drunk, many with 'Three times three', and to the toast:

'"May the success of locomotive power be equal to our most sanguine expectations" . . . Mr. Booth observed, with regard to the particular terms of the toast, that the success of the locomotive power had not only already equalled our

*The last item in a n otebook kept by Mr. Rastrick is a detailed account of the Engineers' Dinner — sixty-one sat down, of whom seventeen were guests, the total cost being £97.16.7.

expectations but exceeded it; and he contemplated the time when the Railway Company should offer premiums for machines which shall as far exceed the present, as these do all that have gone before them. Such an offer would be the means, at least, of again assembling the present company upon a similar cheerful occasion.

'. . . the company separated at as late an hour as propriety would justify at that time of the week, the steam of good fellowship and excellent feeling having been kept up during the whole of the meeting.'*

On Wednesday, the Judges arrived late and the weather being dull and later wet, little was done and there were few spectators. Novelty, Rocket and Sans Pareil were 'exercised' and one of Mr. Brandreth's horses on the Cycloped fell through the floor, but happily was extricated uninjured.

On Thursday, the 8th the Rocket carried out its trials and fulfilled all the conditions demanded of it.**

On weighing, the Rocket was found to be 4 tons 5 cwt and two wagons and the tender brought the total load to be moved to 17 tons. The length of the course, the ends being marked by two posts, was 1½ miles, with ⅛ of a mile at each end for stopping and re-starting, and ten round trips were to be made, being equivalent to the distance between Liverpool and Manchester. Further supplies of coke and water were then to be taken in and the ten round trips repeated, equal to a return journey. The Rocket took 2 hours 14 minutes 8 seconds for the first ten round trips (13.4 miles per hour) with 57 minutes 40 seconds for stopping and re-starting. On the second ten trips the times were 2 hours 6 minutes 49 seconds (14.2 miles per hour) and 50 minutes 20 seconds. On the eastward journey the engine propelled the wagons and pulled them on the return journey. The times on the westward journey were always less than on the eastward one and the last trips were fastest in both experiments; the last westward journey being at over 24 miles per hour, showing that there was a plentiful supply of steam at the end of each part of the trial.

The Albion.
**The Judges' list of conditions is in Appendix III.

According to the *Liverpool Times*, with the frequent starting and stopping of the Rocket many gentlemen had the pleasure of rides mounted behind the engine, Dr. Traill, Mr. Henry Moss and Mr. Robert Gladstone being among their number.

In the *Liverpool Chronicle*'s report of the first day, it criticized the Rocket and said: 'There is nothing new or peculiar in its construction — nothing extraordinary in its first performance. It did not consume its smoke, there being a constant and not inconsiderable column of smoke.' It did not believe that it went at 24 miles an hour, but that it never exceeded 18. It also complained that in the new regulations issued on the 6th October, there was no mention of consuming smoke. Finally, on the eighth day, the newspaper did congratulate Mr. Stephenson 'with all sincerity' on the perfection of 'the old-fashioned engine'. The *Mechanic's Magazine* also mentioned smoke on the first day, but the *Liverpool Times*, in its account, produced a counterblast to the allegations:

'It has been stated that it [the Rocket] emitted very little smoke, but during the trial it emitted none. Previous to the trial a little coal* was put into it and it sent forth smoke, but after the trial commenced it used coke, which, as it does not produce any smoke, could not emit any. We know that there were some persons on the ground who mistook steam for smoke.'

The *Mechanic's Magazine*, in a subsequent number, confirmed that the smoke on the first day was due to some coal being in the coke, but that later in the trial there was no smoke.

The Judges' report to the Directors was only mentioned in the *Liverpool Mercury*, in which, on the 30th October 1829, it stated that the premium of £500 had been awarded to Mr. Henry Booth and the Stephensons, proprietors of the Rocket. In all acounts the Rocket was described as Mr. Robert

---

*The Board ordered that a supply of coal and coke should be provided at the Millfield yard where the engines were prepared.

The Rocket — as rebuilt

Stephenson's locomotive and only in the *Liverpool Times* was it reported that it had a boiler of new construction, adapted for coke, the invention of Mr. Henry Booth, Treasurer of the Railway Company. The consequence of the lack of publicity was that in 1880, when the fiftieth anniversary of the Liverpool & Manchester was celebrated, credit was not given to Henry Booth for his part in the success of the Rocket. As his daughter Mary Anne Booth wrote to the newspapers:

'The "Rocket" engine was built at Stephenson's works in Newcastle, but Henry Booth was the sole inventor of the multitubular boiler, by which a stationary was converted into a locomotive engine. Stephenson acknowledged at once the soundness of the principle, and undertook the construction of the engine. In this way it was the joint work of Stephenson and my father. But in a little while the world, as it is too apt to do, forgot the inventor, and now almost the whole credit of this, the first locomotive engine, is awarded to Stephenson.'*

Various improvements were incorporated into the Rocket, some of them before the opening of the railway in September 1830. The exhaust into the chimney was led into one pipe instead of two which narrowed at the top sharpening the blast and increasing the draught through the fire, an idea obtained from the Sans Pareil. First the chimney was widened so that by removing a cover the tubes could be cleaned from the front of the engine. Then the chimney was replaced by a smoke box with the chimney on top with two doors to open in front,** the top one for cleaning the tubes, the bottom one for removing the ashes. Lastly, the angle of the cylinders was altered to nearly horizontal, as this contributed to smoother running.

Henry Booth's multitubular boiler, used in the Rocket, was the factor which made for the success of the steam locomotive. It was also invented independently in France by M. Marc Seguin of the St. Etienne Railway. He took out a French

Alfred Booth p. 24.
**In an Ackermann print of February 1831 'Entrance of the Railway at Edge Hill, Liverpool' the engine on the left is the Rocket, with a man removing the ashes from the bottom of the smoke box.

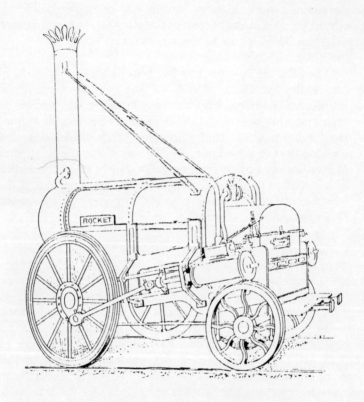

The Rocket – after modification

Patent in February 1828 and in 1829 he was actually having engines built at Robert Stephenson & Company's works in Newcastle. These particular engines had water tubes not fire tubes and were subsequently modified after delivery, because the tubes became blocked by scale. Seguin did not construct a locomotive with a multitubular boiler with fire tubes until after the Rocket, so this engine was the first built to this principle.

In 1865 the French engineer Perdonnet, wrote that the idea may have occurred to two men of genius simultaneously.

In his *Life of George Stephenson* published in 1857, Samuel Smiles quoted from a letter written to him by Henry Booth:

'I am ignorant of M. Seguin's proceedings in France, but claim to be the inventor in England, and . . . that until I named my plan to Mr. Stephenson, with a view to compete for the prize at Rainhill, it had not been tried, and was not known in this country.'

However, the tradition has persisted in France to this day; in a French television programme in 1978 it was mentioned that the multitubular boiler in the Rocket was a French invention.

At the time of the competition there was much grumbling because it was felt that it would be almost impossible to compete with an engine entered by the two principal officers of the Railway, the Engineer and the Treasurer; that the Judges' decision was correct is clear when it is seen what happened to the two main competitors.

The Sans Pareil started its official test on Tuesday, the 13th October. It did not comply with the conditions, as it was too heavy for an engine with four wheels and it had no springs. However, it was allowed to compete, but on the fifth trip there was trouble with the feed water pump; attempts were made to repair it and at the next two stops an extra 8 gallons of water were taken in to the tender each time. On the eighth trip the pump failed and the boiler water level fell so low that the fusible plug melted and put out the fire. It had travelled at an average of nearly 14 miles an hour during the completed trips. It was claimed that part of the trouble was a faulty cylinder cast by Robert Stephenson & Company. This was only

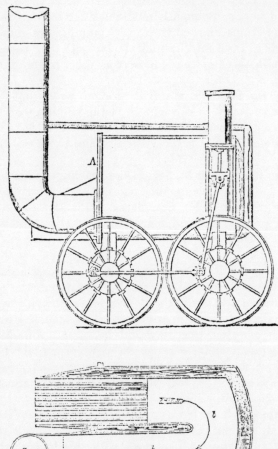

The Sans Pareil

discovered after the trials, and Nicholas Wood, one of the Judges, makes no mention of it in his book *Practical Treatise on Railroads*.*

On the 20th October the Board agreed to Timothy Hackworth's request that it should purchase the Sans Pareil for £550 when it was repaired; George Stephenson estimated that this would take three weeks. It was then hired to the Bolton & Leigh Railway at £15 per week, where it worked, hauling coal trains, until 1840.

The design of the Sans Pareil was, however, never going to be satisfactory for higher speeds. With vertical cylinders and a short wheelbase it would have pitched badly, and been very damaging to the track. John Dixon,** one of George Stephenson's assistants, writing to his brother on the 16th October 1829, said of the Sans Pareil that it rolled about like an empty beer tub on a rough pavement.

The Sans Pareil incorporated one feature, the blast pipe, the invention of Timothy Hackworth, essential to the future development of the multitubular boiler.

The early locomotives had chimneys reaching up to 15 feet or more above the level of the rails. This resulted in a good draught through the fire. An engine driver in the early days of steam locomotives, troubled with the clouds of steam around his engine, is credited with the idea of putting the waste steam from the cylinders up the chimney; it was then observed that at every puff of steam from the cylinders, the fire brightened, so that it became normal practice to use the exhaust steam in this way.

Timothy Hackworth's invention was to reduce the size of the steam pipe at its orifice, which produced a bigger vacuum in the chimney. The vacuum in the Rocket's chimney when tested at Newcastle was only 3″ of water, less than ¼″ of mercury, a quite negligible amount, so that the purchase of the Sans Pareil contributed considerably to the improvement of the Rocket and subsequent engines built to its design. To achieve the best results it is essential to obtain the right balance between getting a good draught on the fire, without excessive

*3rd edition.
**Later L&MR Engineer.

back pressure on the exhaust steam, which reduces the efficiency of the engine. In more recent times, where the blast pipe was designed to get the best results, if an engine steamed badly, it was common practice to restrict the blast pipe orifice, and this was often done by the driver or foreman without authorization.

Crucially Sans Pareil with only 90 square feet of heating surface, compared with the Rocket's 138 square feet, most of which — 118 sq.ft. — came from the more efficient thin copper tubes, a very hot fire and so a fierce blast was needed, which resulted in excessive fuel consumption of coke, nearly 29 lbs of coke being needed to evaporate 1 cubic feet of water, compared with 11¾ lbs for the Rocket.*

The Novelty received far better press publicity at the time. This was partly due to its much neater and less clumsy appearance and lively performance, but also because assisting Braithwaite and Ericsson was the Engineer C.B. Vignoles (1793-1875), who supplied detailed accounts of its performance to the press and *Mechanic's Magazine*.

C.B. Vignoles was the son of an army officer who, with his family, was captured by the French when serving in the West Indies. Both his parents died within a week of each other and, in November 1794, to get the infant back to England he was commissioned and put on half pay at the age of 18 months as an Ensign in the 43rd Foot. He was brought up by his grandfather, and in 1810 went to Sandhurst and then served in the Peninsular War, being present at the battle of Vittoria (1813). In 1814 he was commissioned in the 1st Royal Scots, due to the good offices of the Duke of Kent, and saw service in Holland in that year. In 1816, on half pay, he became a surveyor in Florida and returned to England in 1823. When the Rennies were appointed Engineers for the Liverpool & Manchester Railway Committee in 1825, he was the Engineer who was responsible for the work under their supervision. When the Liverpool & Manchester Railway Bill was passed, Vignoles was engaged, on the 5th June 1826, at £4.4s. a week

*On the Bolton & Leigh Railway the Sans Pareil used coal as its fuel and this reduced the excessive consumption. (L&MR Directors' Minutes 3/10/1831 — when the possibility of selling the Sans Pareil to the Stockton & Darlington Railway was discussed.)

without expenses, to stake out the line and was expecting, in due course, to be responsible for the construction of the line under the Rennies.

When George Stephenson was appointed the Engineer in July, Vignoles remained as his assistant, but clearly the two were incompatible; in any case George Stephenson preferred to employ assistants who had previously worked for him. Eventually Vignoles resigned, in February 1827, when he was given an extra quarter's salary, but he was prejudiced against the Stephensons for many years. In 1830 Vignoles and Ericsson took out a joint patent, and he was obviously closely connected with Braithwaite and Ericsson.

The Novelty was first tested on Saturday, the 10th October, but broke down on the return journey of the first trip. After repairs, it started a new trial on Wednesday, the 14th but on the second trip the pipe carrying the heat through the horizontal boiler collapsed and put the fire out. It was considered at the time that a joint made during the repairs had yielded, but from what they saw of the pipe when taken out of the engine, Stephenson and Locke were satisfied that the pipe was the cause of the failure. The Novelty was then withdrawn.

As the Novelty had been so popular with the public, the L&MR Board decided to give it further consideration. An extra bellows was fitted to ensure a better draught, and the pipe which had failed was lowered to prevent overheating. In the report Henry Booth read to the Shareholders at the Annual Meeting on the 25th March 1830 it was stated that:

'. . . four more [Locomotives] are building . . . . two by Messrs. Braithwaite and Ericsson of London on the principle of the Novelty, but with considerable improvements on that machine, as exhibited at Rainhill in October last. The requisite alterations to this engine occupied several months, and it was not till the 26th January last that the Directors had the opportunity of witnessing a fair experiment. On this occasion the performance was such as in the opinion of the Directors to justify them ordering two larger Engines . . . which will enable them to obtain for these machines the most complete and satisfactory trial.'

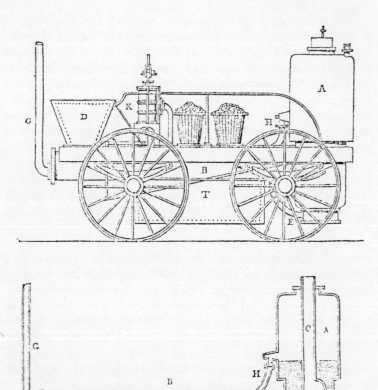

The Novelty

The price was to be £1,000 each; Robert Stephenson & Company charged £550 to £650 for their engines.

In August, Braithwaite and Ericsson received Royal permission to name their engines King William IV and Queen Adelaide.

The engines were expected to be available for the Opening of the Liverpool & Manchester Railway on the 15th September 1830, but although the King William IV reached Manchester before that date, it was not in working order. It travelled to Liverpool on the 22nd September and on the 23rd it was seen 'exercising' there by a correspondent of the *Liverpool Chronicle*. On the 24th on the return journey, it was de-railed. On the 30th August, George Stephenson had reported that the wheels were loose — set for a narrower gauge than 4'8½" — the cause of the accident, which delayed traffic on Saturday, the 25th September. Afterwards permission was given for it to travel only between Manchester and Eccles after the last train had departed. In January 1831, it was expected to be ready shortly, but after that there is no mention of Braithwaite and Ericsson's engines in the L&MR Board Minutes.

At about this time C.B. Vignoles was building the St. Helens and Runcorn Gap (Widnes) Railway, and the three engines, Novelty, King William IV and Queen Adelaide were transferred to that railway. In one of Ackermann's prints of the Liverpool & Manchester Railway dated 1832, one of the two latter engines is seen with a train crossing the bridge over the L&MR line, but there is no record of how long they actually worked.

The design of these engines was compact and neat, but there was no future for it, as it was impossible to clean the inside of the tube in the horizontal boiler through which the heat was passed. Mr. Laird inspected the Novelty during the Rainhill Trials and had commented on how clean the tube was at the end near the grate. However, it was the two U bends further along the tube which were likely to cause trouble. With the multitubular boiler it was easy to clean the tubes once the smoke box door was fitted. Another problem, the very strong draught from the bellows needed to force the air through the narrow pipe in the horizontal boiler, produced a very hot fire likely to cause excessive heating at the start of the pipe.

Through the trials there were no accidents, although numerous people travelled on the engines and, in spite of the constables, the crowds encroached on the line, particularly on the first day. On the Saturday, a man was run over by the Sans Pareil, but with great presence of mind he lay flat between the rails and escaped uninjured.

Mr. Rastrick's fee, including attendance and expenses, was £199.5.10d. The account was not sent in until March 1831 and on the 7th of that month the L&MR Board ordered its payment. Mr. Wood's fee was £151.15.7d. and this was paid on the 8th February 1830. Mr. Kennedy, a wealthy cotton spinner and inventor, received no payment.

The price of Liverpool & Manchester Railway £100 shares which had fallen from £150 in December 1828 to £116 in July 1829, rose from £137 in August to £150 after the trials.

In a letter to the *Liverpool Mercury* on the 30th October 1829 'A Doubter' wrote:

'. . . Another consideration belonging to this steam affair is the enormous consumption of fuel it occasions.

'The sellers of coal tell you their mines are inexhaustible: in this they may be wrong; and I see no right that the present generation has to waste that which those who succeed us may want, a hundred or even a thousand years hence.'

According to Professor W.A. Tuplin, in his book *The Steam Locomotive* (1974)

'The design of the Rocket's boiler represented perhaps the biggest single technological advance in the history of the steam locomotive. With one modification it formed the model for all subsequent locomotive boilers.'

Chapter VI

The Directors' Report for the Annual General Meeting of the 25th March 1830 dealt with the consequences of the Rainhill contest, one of these being the need to provide for a large passenger traffic:

'The Directors have provided a Coach Manufactory, and have made arrangements to have completed, by the end of June, Engines and Coaches for the conveyance of a thousand passengers per day, between Liverpool and Manchester; though they are by no means sanguine enough to expect to carry so large a number in the first instance. The Company have six Locomotives employed, four more are building.'

Henry Booth was interested in the reduction of friction in order to take full advantage of the use of rails and the Report continued:

'Whilst the Directors have used every exertion to obtain the most complete and unexceptionable moving power, they have at the same time been anxious to ascertain and to adopt the best construction of Waggons and Carriages. Various schemes for diminishing the friction of Wheels and Axles have been proposed, and have received due attention. A new system of Friction Wheels, the invention of Mr. Winans, an American gentleman, claimed the most consideration; and the Directors purchased from Mr. Winans a dozen of his Carriages as an experiment.'

As has been mentioned, Mr. Winans had demonstrated one of these, a hand driven wagon, at Rainhill. Mr. Winans' system, which involved the axles running in oil baths, while sound in theory, when tested had proved inferior to the plain greased bearings used by the Stephensons. The tests were carried out by Mr. Rastrick and the Dock Board's surveyor, Mr. Hartley, by letting wagons run down the Whiston Incline and seeing how far they went on the level from its foot. At the same time, some patent bearings invented by Dr. Brandreth, a former L&MR Director, were tried, but these were even less satisfactory than those of Mr. Winans.

While the intention was to give a more extensive trial to the twelve wagons — [not carriages] — purchased from Mr. Winans, the bearings were very easily damaged and the wagons needed to be put in order before the trial could take place. Here the Directors came up against a great unwillingness to do the work. George Stephenson refused to have anything to do with the wagons, and when Mr. William Brown, an outside Engineer, was asked to carry out the repairs, he pointed out that it was a waste of money to do so. Mr. Winans was paid for his wagons — £285.9.7. He was also given the sum of £50 by the Directors as compensation; due to some error, Mr. Winans, an alien, had been detained in prison for several days.

During this period Henry Booth wrote *An Account of the Liverpool and Manchester Railway.** It was published in June 1830 and there was a second edition in 1831. The book was also published in America and a translation appeared in France. In the *Account*, with the permission of the Directors, full details were given of the expenditure on the Railway to date.

The following quotations from the last chapter of his book clearly define Henry Booth's vision of a better world:

'But perhaps the most striking result produced by the

*In 1969 the book was re-published in a facsimile edition.

completion of this Railway, is the sudden and marvellous change which has been effected in our ideas of time and space. Notions which we have received from our ancestors, and verified by our own experience, are overthrown in a day, and a new standard erected, by which to form our ideas for the future. Speed — despatch — distance — are still relative terms, but their meaning has been totally changed within a few months: what was quick is now slow; what was distant is now near; and this change in our ideas will not be limited to the environs of Liverpool and Manchester — it will pervade society at large . . . .

'The genius of Watt, or Davy, or Stephenson, may improve the state of nations, or the fortunes of individuals, but it affects not the condition of the great mass of the human race; for this consummation we must look to other sciences than chemistry and mechanics; to the tardy overthrow of prejudice, and the slow progress of unpopular truth; to the diffusion of that knowledge which teaches the laws and principles on which depend the moral, physical, and political condition, the subsistence, and well-being of mankind.

'Meanwhile, the genius of the age, like a mighty river of the new world, flows onward, full, rapid, and irresistible. The spirit of the times must needs manifest itself in the progress of events, and the movement is too impetuous to be stayed, were it wise to attempt it. Like the "Rocket" of fire and steam, or its prototype of war and desolation — whether the harbinger of peace and the arts, or the Engine of hostile attack and devastation — though it be a futile attempt to oppose so mighty an impulse, it may not be unworthy our ambition, to guide its progress and direct its course.'

It is remarkable that this *Account* was written in June 1830, before the opening of the railway, and when only one trip to Manchester, described at the end of the book, had been made. The journey, which took place on the 14th June, was reported in the *Liverpool Mercury*. The weather was wet, but there were large crowds at all vantage points to watch the train pass, a foretaste of the opening three months later. The Directors and Henry Booth partook of a cold collation at the house of one of the Marquis of Stafford's representative Directors, Mr. G. Winter, who lived in Manchester. 'The engine which drew the train was on the same principle as the Rocket which gained the prize at Rainhill, with the boiler designed by Henry Booth, and with improvements made by the Company's engineers and the manufacturers Robert Stephenson & Company.'

A committee of Directors was appointed to arrange the opening ceremony, and in July the Duke of Wellington, the Prime Minister, accepted the invitation of the committee to be the principal guest.

In July there was the revolution in France in which King Charles X was replaced by the Duke of Orleans, Louis Philippe. In Liverpool a fund was established for the benefit of the people of Paris who had resisted the tyranny. A public meeting* was held at which the first speaker was the Rev. W. Shepherd, who was in the chair. Henry Booth seconded the resolution, reported in the *Liverpool Mercury*, in the following words:

'It was more incumbent on Englishmen to mark their abhorrence of that most atrocious attempt to enslave high spirited people. (Applause) He warmly eulogized the spirit, moderation and magnanimity displayed by the people of Paris, as showing them to be worthy of liberty, and as teaching monarchs that they only reigned for the good of their subjects, and that the people were the only source and sanction of power. (Great Applause)'

These events in France resulted in fears of similar disturbances in this country, and when, owing to the acciaent to Mr. Huskisson, there was a delay in the trains reaching Manchester on the opening day, it caused considerable anxiety. Newspapers reported that some of the crowd waved tricolour flags with cries of 'Vote by ballot' and 'No Corn Laws', and hissed and booed when the Duke of Wellington passed.

*This was held on the 14th August. First reports of the fighting between the 26th and 29th July gave the number killed as 6,000 to 8,000. It later became clear that the figures had been greatly exaggerated.

A description of the Opening of the Railway on the 15th September is given in the following extract from a letter written to her sister in Hampstead by Mrs. Thomas Fletcher. Her daughter Emily had married Henry Booth's youngest brother Charles the previous year.

'You have heard that yesterday was to be our grand opening of the railway. You probably know that Mr. Henry Kinder gave us his ticket. You will doubtless hear immediately that there has been an accident to poor Mr. Huskisson, and it will be a satisfaction to you to know that the user of the ticket, and Charles and Emily, who also went, have not been in the slightest difficulty, and that there was no other accident the whole day to the engines or to the immense multitude, but this dreadful one. The day was fine, the carriages and company perfect, the scene magnificent, the crowds immense. They went off in the finest style, the populace delighted and, as Emily describes it, every face was smiling and beaming with joy and satisfaction. In this way they went on about nineteen miles, not too rapidly that all might be safe, the whole way lined with people and stands and booths filled with all the surrounding gentry. There are two roads for carriages on the railway (I believe you saw it); on one went the military band, the Duke,* great people and directors, on the other all the rest, about 700 or 800 altogether. When they got to this place the Duke's steam-engine stopped to take on more water — other carriages were coming after at a distance — some of the gentlemen in the Duke's carriage got out, and Mr. Huskisson went round to speak to some ladies, and came to the side which was next to the other road. Seeing another carriage coming, the door was opened for him to get in, but whether the door slipped from his hand, or whether in his agitation he lost his footing, is not known, but he fell and one leg was caught by the machine and greatly fractured. Had he remained standing he could not have been injured, but it is supposed he lost his presence of mind, and thus threw himself into danger. The scene was

*Duke of Wellington.

most distressing and agitating to everybody. He called out to
be left to die there, no doubt feeling dreadfully injured. The
military car was attached to one of the engines and the poor
man laid upon it, and with Mrs. Huskisson, Lord Wilton,
three medical men, and two or three more friends, was
conveyed at the speed of thirty miles an hour to Eccles, to
the Parsonage Home where Mr. Blackburn resided, who
was known to some of the party, and whose house was close
to the railroad. There was now a general delay; for two
hours there was a debate whether to go back to Liverpool or
go on to Manchester; the Duke and Sir Robert Peel, who
were both greatly affected, declared they could go no
further, and everybody felt and expressed that it would be a
relief to return, but it was considered by the Directors and
by all the influential men, that it would be a ruinous
discredit to the whole undertaking if they did not proceed to
Manchester, and that it would be impossible to say what the
effect of the disappointment might be to the assembled
multitude at Manchester: so they determined to go on, but
with what changed feelings! Every face was sad, no military
band was with them, no bugles sounded, and the shouts as
they passed had no return. Emily says nothing was ever so
shocking or affecting as this contrast. When they arrived
within five miles of Manchester the mob, weary of waiting,
had actually filled the whole of the railroad, and to avoid
crushing myriads they could only move at a snail's pace, and
the noise and shouts and confusion were beyond everything,
for neither policemen nor soldiers could resist the dense
crowd.

'At Manchester warehouses were prepared with a cold
collation, but before the Liverpool party arrived many had
got in without tickets, and the numbers made it most
bewildering. In consequence of the engines being sent off
with Mr. Huskisson, and for surgeons, and in consequence
of the impossibility of moving rapidly along to fetch fresh
water, there was considerable delay at Manchester, and
several of the carriages did not get back till ten at night,
Emily and Charles of the number; but thank God she is no
worse and must after this be called, well; we were dreadfully
uneasy. We heard a rumour in the evening that Mr.

Huskisson was hurt, then that his leg was broken, then that he was so much injured that he could not recover, and the unexpected lateness of the return of the carriages (for five was the latest talked of) made us dread everything. However, they came safe at last, and we hoped the morning would bring happier news of the poor sufferer; but this morning we found that he died last night about nine.

'I cannot describe to you the horror and grief of everybody here. Our member, a man beloved by all parties, looked up to by the nation — his wife by his side — surrounded by friends interested in him, everything conspires to render the blow shocking and awful. Nothing is spoken of today but this. Every face wears a settled gloom. The shops are half-shut — the Duke is gone — the festivities all put a stop to — Mr. F. [Fletcher] was to have dined with the Mayor and Corporation today in the grand assembly room, and to have been in a steamboat on the river this morning with the Duke; and there was to have been a ball to-night, and the Duke was to have dined with the Town on Saturday; but it is right that all is given up, and it is right that such an awful dispensation should be felt by everybody. I sincerely hope that this afflicting accident will not injure the concern, and that no blame will attach to the engineers. The distress of engineers and directors is, you may believe, very great indeed — but whatever delay or difficulty there was afterwards is also entirely attributable to the delay, loss of engines, and confusion which the accident created — and it is thought by everybody that if it had not happened, all would have gone well through the day.

'Is it not surprising that Mr. Huskisson should have gone into a situation where there was a possibility of danger, and more especially when he was delicate, and one leg numb since his last illness — I would send you a Liverpool paper today, but the edition is all sold up . . . .'

On the Thursday after the opening, a train was run from Liverpool to Manchester for a special party. On the Friday, a passenger service of three trains each way was started, trains departing from Liverpool and Manchester at 7 a.m., noon and 4 p.m. A few days later the service was increased to four trains each way, two First Class and two Second Class, as this enabled the train crews to make one return journey each day. In addition, every day a return trip was run to Sankey Viaduct, one of the outstanding achievements on the railway, using the special carriage in which the Duke of Wellington had travelled at the opening ceremony.

On the 18th October, the Directors made a rule that unauthorized persons should not be permitted to ride on the engine. It is well known that George Stephenson gave Fanny Kemble, the actress, a ride on an engine in June 1830 and clearly others had repeated this exploit. The Directors, the Treasurer, George Stephenson and five assistant engineers were allowed to ride on engines without special permission.

Owing to the shortage of engine power, due to the failure of Braithwaite and Ericsson to deliver their engines, only passenger traffic was attempted in the first instance. At the beginning of 1831 goods traffic started when more engines had arrived from Robert Stephenson & Company. The Board met constantly to deal with day to day problems, but the increase of the traffic necessitated the formation of a Management Committee* to consider these in more detail than could be done by the Board. One of the duties of the committee was to check the bills from the engineering department which were due for payment. The committee met every other Thursday, but occasionally it became necessary to meet up to three times a week. It met at the Treasurer's office at Crown Street Station, or at the general office in North John Street, where the engineering accounts were kept, and on occasion in the Board Room at Clayton Square.

The railway was naturally Henry Booth's principal concern, but he continued to take an active part in politics until the passing of the Municipal Reform Bill in 1835.

On the 27th April 1831 there was a meeting in the Music Hall at noon attended by 3,000 people, to approve an Address to His Majesty King William IV for having dissolved Parliament. The first resolution, proposed by Mr. W.W. Currie, was seconded by Henry Booth, and the following is taken from the *Liverpool Mercury*'s report on his speech:

*After the 5th April 1832 called the Sub-Committee.

'The King and his Ministers had nobly done their duty — it remained for the people to do theirs. (Cheers) It had been usual to style His Majesty's Ministers the King's servants, it would now be more correct to call them the servants of the people . . . He had just returned from town, and whilst there he saw His Majesty come down in person to prorogue the Parliament, by which act he had enthroned himself in the hearts of the people. (Applause) His Majesty had proved himself to be a patriot King, and all they could do in return was, to prove themselves a loyal and devoted people. (Cheers)'

Shortly before the dissolution, Mr. William Ewart, a Reformer, who had been elected to succeed Mr. Huskisson in 1830, had been unseated because of corrupt practices in the election. The election was declared void and Mr. Ewart not duly elected. For years Liverpool had been notorious for corrupt electoral practices, particularly in the Mayoral Election of 1827. To avoid these in the ensuing General Election on the 3rd and 4th May, extra polling booths were provided. This resulted in polling being completed in ten hours, compared with the six days the previous election had lasted. General Gascoyne, who was opposed to Parliamentary Reform, was not elected and a Conservative, Mr. Denison, who was stated to be in favour of it, was elected with Mr. Ewart.* A few days later Mr. Denison was also elected a member for Nottinghamshire, and decided not to take up the Liverpool seat, whereupon a further election became necessary. At the end of May, in the hope that the writ would be issued, the Reformers in Liverpool chose Mr. Thomas Thornely as their candidate. Mr. William Brown proposed the nomination, and this was seconded by Henry Booth. The *Liverpool Times* reported that:

'Mr. Henry Booth assured the meeting that he had great pleasure in seconding the nomination of Mr. Thornely. He had known that gentleman intimately upwards of twenty

---

*The candidates received the following votes: Ewart 1,919, Denison 1,890 and Gascoyne 607. Mr. Denison did vote for the Reform Bill.

years, and, during all that time, he had found him
consistent and true to his principle as a friend of civil and
religious liberty, as an advocate of free trade, and as the
determined and persevering opposer of all commercial
monopolies. (Great applause) He had found him uniformly
anxious to promote a reciprocity of good feeling, not only
between man and man, but between nation and nation.
(Applause) During the whole period of their acquaintance,
he had found Mr. Thornely a constant and active supporter
of the great measure of Parliamentary Reform. (Great
applause) . . . if they elected him as their representative in
Parliament, he had the most perfect confidence that they
would find no reason whatsoever to repent of their choice.
(Great applause).'

The Liverpool writ was eventually issued in October 1831.
Lord Sandon, who had come forward to represent the
Conservative interest in place of General Gascoyne, was
nominated and seconded by Charles Lawrence and John Moss.
After Mr. Thornely had been nominated, the election was
postponed until the next day to enable new arrangements to be
made for the polling, which had to be conducted more rapidly
than in previous elections; under the Liverpool Disenfranchise-
ment Bill, the poll had to last not more than three days.
According to the *Liverpool Mercury*:

'At the conclusion of the business at the hustings, both
parties adjourned to their different places of rendezvous,
accompanied by flags, banners, and bands of music. Mr.
Thornely and his friends proceeded to a house opposite the
Adelphi Hotel, in Ranelagh-square, where a strong
platform had been prepared for the accommodation of the
speakers.'

Mr. Thornely addressed the 'assembled multitude' and, the
Liverpool Mercury reported:

'Mr. Henry Booth then came forward, and said that the
time was now come for the freemen of the town of Liverpool
to show what they were made of, and decide whether they

would elect as their representative a Noble Lord drawn
from the high places of the aristocracy; or a free, intelligent
and independent merchant, taken from amongst themselves. (Applause) Lord Sandon had that day told the
freemen on the hustings that he felt himself to be unfit to
represent the interests of this great commercial place. ("So
he is," — much laughter and applause) Why, then, did his
Lordship come forward at all? His Lordship had not
answered this question, but he hoped that his Lordship
would take an early opportunity of doing so, to the
satisfaction of the freemen. (Applause)

'Mr. Thornely had reminded them at the hustings that it
was not very long since they have been represented by two
military officers, who had passed through the town with red
coats and cockades, as representatives of the intelligence of
Liverpool; he asked them whether that would be borne at
the present day. ("No, no!") He had no doubt that in a few
years it would be thought quite as inconsistent that an
hereditary peer should represent the interests of this great
town, as that two military officers should be sent to
Parliament from Liverpool. (Applause) A great change had
taken place in the minds of men from the advancing
intelligence of the age. If they looked into the dictionary
they would find that the word representative meant an exact
likeness of themselves. Now was Lord Sandon, or could he
ever be the likeness of themselves? If Lord Sandon should be
returned, what could he represent? He put this question for
the sake of information. Would his Lordship represent the
wants and wishes of the industrious people of Liverpool, or
did he possess the commercial knowledge and experience
necessary to enable him to be the representative of
mercantile men? ("No, no!" — and applause)

'In the name of wonder, then, what would Lord Sandon
represent? It might be said, that he would represent the
politics of the party which supported him, but this he
doubted, for it was impossible to say what those politics
were. (Laughter and cheers) He advised them, therefore, to
elect Mr. Thornely as their representative, not for Mr.
Thornely's advantage but for their own good. (Applause)
They ought to fix their choice on Mr. Thornely, because

they know him to be an upright and intelligent merchant, both willing and able to support and promote the best interests of the town. (Cheers) On these grounds he came forward and solicited their votes for Mr. Thornely at the ensuing election. (Loud cheers)'

Polling started at 10 a.m. the next day. At 3.10 p.m. Mr. Thornely conceded the contest,* Lord Sandon having received 1,519 votes to his 670.

In July 1832 the Reform Bill was passed and on the 4th September a public dinner to celebrate the event was held in the Royal Amphitheatre in Great Charlotte Street. Henry Booth and his brother Thomas were stewards, as well as seven who were or had been Directors of the L&MR. Tickets were 15/- each, including admission to the boxes for one lady. The entrance for the ladies was in Great Charlotte Street, and the gentlemen were to enter by the pit door, which was to be open at 5.30 p.m. and take their seats. Gentlemen were not to be admitted to the boxes.

The Rev. W. Shepherd was in the chair, and in proposing the toast to Mr. William Ewart, the Reformer Member of Parliament for Liverpool, he said:

'I stand in need of quiet and repose. It is, therefore, my determination that this shall be the last time of my presiding at a political dinner.'**

The *Liverpool Journal* reported:

'The Rev. W. Shepherd filled the chair with his accustomed ease and dignity. He spoke well and did not appear to speak more than was required of him; but still he hardly left any room for the incidental admission of any speech but his own.'

*After the Reform Bill, Mr. Thornely contested the 1832 Election in Liverpool, and although on the second day he was second to Mr. Ewart with over 3,000 votes, on the third day he was overtaken by Lord Sandon, who polled 4,154 votes to Mr. Thornely's 4,013 votes; Lord Sandon being elected with Mr. Ewart. In 1835 Mr. Thornely was elected Member of Parliament for Wolverhampton.
**The *Liverpool Times*.

Before leaving the dinner at 10.45 p.m. the Rev. Shepherd appointed Mr. P. Woods to take the chair. The *Liverpool Mercury* reported that the company:

> 'Kept up the sacrifice to Bacchus for some time longer. Not the slightest unpleasant circumstance occurred during the whole evening, not an angry or hasty word was spoken and the whole passed off with the greatest harmony and good humour and that is more than we can say of almost any public dinner we ever attended.'

Henry Booth wrote a pamphlet 'Free Trade as it affects the people: Addressed to a Reformed Parliament'. It was published in Liverpool in January 1833 and cost 1½d. After pointing out the advantages of free trade, he considered how the Government could make good the loss of revenue due to the abolishment of customs duties. Once again he looked forward to a better world ensuing from the peace and good feeling between nations as well as laying the foundations of lasting prosperity for the country. The pamphlet ends with the words:

> 'Legislation must acquire a new spirit and our rulers a higher aim. Every proceeding of Government must be for the permanent well being of the people. Under such influences it would be difficult to prescribe limits to the career of prosperity, which this country may be destined to run.
>
> 'When we contemplate the varied capabilities of the British people; their knowledge, their enterprise, their capital, their manufacturing skill, their indefatigable industry, their infinite perseverance, the mineral riches of the kingdom, what is required to impart the first great impulse to these mighty elements, is that the iron hand of power shall not paralyse their own and the nation's welfare.'

After the election of the Reformed Parliament in December 1832, the Whigs, who had passed the Bill, were divided on their next steps. The more radical members looked for more reforms — of the Church, the House of Lords, Local

Government, the Corn Laws and in Ireland. The Government was equally divided in its views, and its members inclined to quarrel amongst themselves. There were repeated crises and threats by individual ministers to resign. In November, Lord Melbourne, who had become Prime Minister in June, resigned. King William, who had become alarmed at the disturbances in the country, asked the Duke of Wellington to form a Government; Sir Robert Peel, the Conservative leader, was on holiday in Italy.

This created an outcry throughout the country and at noon on the 24th November there was a great public meeting in Clayton Square; according to the *Liverpool Mercury* 15,000* were present. Viscount Molyneux was in the chair and after he had made a short speech, Mr. W.W. Currie moved the first resolution, and was reported in *The Albion* as saying:

'The Noble Lord had got his steam up to so high a pressure that it could be difficult for him to keep pace with his Lordship's locomotive. (Loud laughter)'

The resolution was seconded by Colonel Williams, who was now Member of Parliament for Ashton-under-Lyne. Henry Booth moved the second resolution and according to the account in *The Albion*:

'He ridiculed the assurance that the Duke of Wellington would turn Reformer. Can the panther change his skin or a leopard his spots? (Cheers) The people of England did not want a great military commander for their Home Secretary. (Laughter) He agreed with the Tories that sudden changes in Government were dangerous, and in accordance with this maxim let them leave the Reform Bill to its natural working. The people had lately gained power through that Bill, and they should not rest satisfied till they had gained all the constitutional blessings which that modern Magna Carta was capable of conferring. (Immense cheering)'

---

*A report on another occasion stated that 7,000 was the capacity of Clayton Square.

In January 1835 there was a General Election and although there were some Conservative gains and Sir Robert Peel became Prime Minister, he resigned in April and Lord Melbourne formed an administration which brought in the Municipal Reform Bill. This having passed through all its stages in the Commons, went to the House of Lords. The attitude of the Lords was to reject bills of which they disapproved, and in an endeavour to secure the passage of the Bill, protest meetings were held all over the country.

The *Liverpool Times* reported on a meeting held in Clayton Square on the 10th August. The Square was full with between 6,000 and 7,000 people. Colonel Williams was in the chair, and Henry Booth moved the third resolution 'That the House of Lords was ignorant of the opinion of the people'. The following is taken from the newspaper's report of his speech:

'He was surprised at the extraordinary violence and rancour with which the Noble Lords discussed the merits of the Corporation Reform Bill. Sir Robert Peel, leader of the Tory party, was in agreement with the great principle of the Bill, the introduction of a representative system into Municipal Corporations. How were they then to account for the different conduct of the House of Lords? The explanation was not difficult. Corrupt Corporations were the last stronghold of corrupt Toryism. (Cheers) If, therefore, there were any doubts of the necessity of Municipal Reform, there could be none now. He considered this institution the particular province of the people — why should the Noble Lords with so much bitterness interfere? There was too much of that democratic spirit afloat in the country. The people were sufficiently unreasonable to want to have something to do in the management of their own affairs. The House of Lords had done much to alienate the affections and provoke the temper of the people; but let them not urge matters too far . . . . Let them bear in mind that no institution can long subsist that is not in harmony with the spirit of the age, especially no institutions claiming to be an integral part of the Government and constitution of a free country can long survive the well founded hostility, much less the contempt of a whole people. (Loud and continued cheers)'

This appears to be the last speech Henry Booth made in connection with the Reform Movement. The House of Lords passed the Bill with some amendments and the first Reformed Municipal Elections were held at the end of the year.

Chapter VII

At the start of operation of the railway, with only four trains in each direction, the major problems were due to the lack of experience of the staff and the passengers. The dangers of attempting to board or alight from moving trains were not realized, and this resulted in a number of accidents. There were also trespassers. The Treasurer reported to the Board on the 9th April 1834 that a train had run over and killed a man who had been walking, balancing himself on one rail, in Olive Mount Cutting.

As construction work on parts of the line was still in progress, it was necessary to check that the running lines were clear of tools and other obstructions and on the 11th October 1830 the Board had given instructions that:

> 'A pilot engine was to be sent from Liverpool with a good lamp to meet the train from Manchester at 4 p.m. and the same from Manchester for the Liverpool train.'

It appears that the pilots were sent out to meet the two trains on the same track; such a procedure would not have been permitted a few years later.

On the 9th December, the Meteor on the Manchester train was derailed at Elton Head by some wagons on the line; the pilot, the Rocket, being a mile instead of a quarter of a mile ahead. The Rocket, '. . . came back and rescued the train after one hour.' On the 13th the driver of the Rocket, M. Wakefield, appeared before the Board and was told not to get more than a quarter of a mile ahead in future. This was a very mild rebuke compared with the severe line taken with offenders in later years.

On the 13th June 1831, the Treasurer reported to the Board that the first train from Bolton had arrived at Liverpool that morning. Until the Bolton & Leigh Railway was absorbed by the L&MR in 1845, it was worked by a contractor, Mr. Hargreaves, who ran a number of Bolton trains to both Liverpool and Manchester. As a result there was an increase in the number of trains on the line, and the L&MR had less control over the qualifications of the drivers and guards, or the mechanical condition of the rolling stock.

On the 20th November 1831, a Sunday, Mr. John Moss travelled by the 8 a.m. train from Manchester to Liverpool. On the following day he described his journey to the Board. The 15¾ miles to Newton took thirty-five minutes, where a stop of seven minutes was made, which was far too long. The second half of the journey took fifty-five minutes, and stops were made at Kendricks Cross* and Huyton; the Bolton train, which was following, came much too close at these stops.

The Management Committee was asked to look into the matter, and this was done two days later. It was discovered that it had become a custom on Sundays** for drivers and guards to change trains when they passed each other at Newton, as this enabled them to spend most of the day at home; they would otherwise have had to wait in Liverpool or Manchester to take the return trains back at 5 or 6 p.m. This system was approved by the Committee so long as passengers were not inconvenienced. It was ordered that the exchanges were to be made wherever the trains passed, so avoiding a long stop at Newton. This arrangement was later confirmed in a rule reading:

'Some of the enginemen having doubted the practice of

---

*Later Rainhill Station.
**The L&MR was not permitted to run trains on Sundays during the hours of church services. The Treasurer had to calculate the profit on Sunday trains, so that shareholders objecting to Sunday travel could, if they wished, give their share of the profit to charity.

changing engines (half-way) on Sundays was by order, or by permission; notice is given that the enginemen are required to change (half-way) on Sundays, unless by mutual agreement and consent each engineman remains with his own engine.'

The extra stops made by the train at Kendricks Cross and at Huyton were due to the blue train* being just ahead; it had been delayed by snow on the line at Chat Moss, so that both trains moved and stopped together.

The Committee instructed the Treasurer to complain to Mr. Hargreaves about the driving of the Bolton train.

In the previous week Henry Booth wrote a letter to the *Liverpool Times* to contradict an alarming account which appeared in the *Liverpool Mercury* on the 11th November of an incident on the 5th of the month. It was reported that what might have been a very serious accident had occurred on the previous Saturday on the L&MR. An account by a passenger, who was a regular traveller by the railway, and a respectable acquaintance of the Editor, described how, due to the breakage of a wheel on one of the carriages, the whole train was derailed while crossing an embankment at 20 m.p.h. Owing to the softness of the ground it stopped in about 600 yards, just before it would have gone over the edge of the embankment. Providentially, no passenger received the slightest injury. After an hour's delay, the train was again started and:

'. . . in order to make up lost time, the engines were put to their full speed, (notwithstanding the alarm and remonstrances of the passengers, particularly the females some of whom fainted) and performed the distance to Liverpool about 11 miles in 22 minutes.'

The *Liverpool Mercury*'s informant said that on examining the broken wheel, he found that it was made of cast iron, a brittle material, and the paper commented that a precisely

---

*Blue trains were Second Class stopping trains composed mainly of open carriages painted blue.

similar accident had happened a month or two before. The railway had then stated that means had been adopted to prevent such accidents. The *Mercury* suggested the placing of a barrier at the edge of embankments and that trains should reduce speed when travelling across them.

Four days later the letter from Henry Booth '. . . to correct a most erroneous statement in the *Mercury* . . .' appeared in the *Liverpool Times*, and continued:

'Now instead of the whole train being forced off the rails, only the first two coaches left the rails and were held in the correct line of road by the engine *before*, and the other coaches *behind*, which did not leave the rails, the whole story . . . is pure fiction. . . . although the wheel was of cast iron . . . it was bound round with a *wrought* iron tire; the circumstances of these forged iron tires breaking, is one of those rare accidents that might happen to a mail or coach on the common road, with this difference that the railway coaches are linked together by several chains, (three at each end) so that they are held together upright even if a wheel does break. The precisely similar accident was something quite different, the breaking of a crank axle — the Company is now making them stronger and trust they will be perfect. One part of the statement is correct that no one received the slightest injury.'

On the 17th April 1836, a Sunday, an accident happened at Bury Lane to the 5 p.m. First Class train from Liverpool, hauled by the engine Patentee. The minutes of the Directors' meeting next day record that, '. . . the front axle [of the engine] broke when the train crossed over to the South side and ran down the slope into the field pulling two coaches after her.' The engine and coaches were only slightly damaged, and no one was hurt.

Henry Booth was asked to make a report* on the accident. In this he pointed out that the Patentee was the only six-wheeled engine owned by the railway incorporating Robert Stephenson's patented idea of having no flanges on the driving

*PRO file Rail 371 - 12.

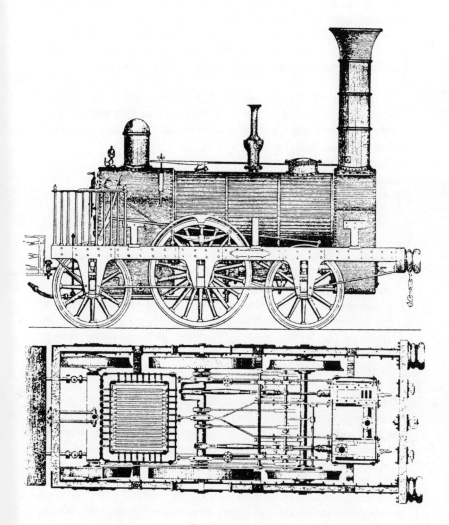

The Patentee

wheels; this made the engine better for going round corners, but meant that the breakage of one of the other axles would derail the engine. He continued that it was desirable to have some protection on embankments in the form of safety mounds, echoing the *Mercury*'s suggestion of 1831. His recommendation was to build mounds on embankments over ten feet high, and detailed the places where surplus earth could be found for this purpose. He ended by writing:

'The New Railways will have their Embankments secured with Fences and Mounds; and *Safety* on the Liverpool and Manchester Railway should not be less efficiently provided for, than on other lines.'

In his book *Railways of Great Britain* (1840), Francis Whishaw wrote about the L&MR:

'The Railway over embankments is generally protected with earth banks, properly sodded. This plan was originally adopted to check the progress of an engine which might get off the rails, but is not followed in railways of more recent date: although we are of opinion that it would be an example worthy of imitation in the lofty embankments of the main lines in the kingdom, if only to afford to the traveller an appearance of safety, although the reason already given is of sufficient importance to cause their general adoption.'

In November 1832 a more serious accident occurred in fog at Rainhill; the 7.15 a.m. Second Class train from Manchester had stopped in the station to pick up a few passengers, when it was run into by the 8 a.m. First Class train, which had only stopped at Newton. The Annual Register described the accident in the following words:

'Fortunately the managers of the stationary train contrived to get it into motion, by which the force of the concussion was in some degree diminished. The concussion was, however, dreadful. The engine of the advancing train struck the hindmost carriage, and, after driving some of them off the road, was driven with tremendous violence against the station house at the side of the road, the front of which was completely carried away. One young man was killed upon the spot. The last carriage of this part being broken to pieces; the next a closed carriage was not much injured; the next three were all more or less so; but the engine and tender escaped without damage. Several of the passengers were most severely hurt, and hardly one escaped without cuts, bruises or contusions.'

This accident resulted in the making of a rule:*

'That whenever a coach-train stops at any of the stations or places for taking up or setting down passengers (during a fog or in thick weather), the gateman or policeman of the station shall immediately run 400 yards behind the train, or so far as may be necessary, to warn any coming engine, in order to prevent its running against the other; and that all enginemen shall slacken speed in foggy weather, and proceed at a slow pace at an ample distance from trains as they approach each of the stations and stopping places, in order that they may have the complete control of, and be able to stop their engines and trains without risk of running against any train which may happen to be waiting at such station or stopping place. And that, in case any engine (whether with coaches or luggage-wagons, or without) shall stop, in foggy or thick weather, in any part of the road where there shall be no gatemen or policemen, and where there shall be no plate-layer to render assistance, the fireman shall immediately run back 400 yards, or so far as may be necessary to warn and stop any other engine coming in the same direction. . . .'

In March 1833 the Board approved a list of Rules and Regulations for Drivers and Guards, with a code of signals, including the following:

'By Day. — The red flag is the signal to stop. . . . It is to

---

*The Appendix to Whishaw's book is the source for the 1839 L&MR Rules.

H

be understood that any flag or lamp, of whatever colour, violently waved, is a signal to stop.

'By Night. — The white light stationary indicates that all is right; but if waved up and down, is a signal to stop; . . . The red light is a signal always to stop. The green light is a signal that a necessity exists to proceed slowly and cautiously; . . .'

The rules were revised from time to time and in the autumn of 1840, the L&MR Board, to allay public anxiety over the number of railway accidents, organized a Conference of Chairman and Managers of the principal railways; the aim being that all lines should profit from the experience of others. Henry Booth had always been responsible for the drafting of the L&MR rules and acted as Secretary of the meeting. A sub-committee of Hardman Earle and Theodore Rathbone revised the rules for the Conference, which was held at Birmingham on the 19th January 1841 and the regulations they put forward were approved by the meeting. They were the L&MR rules, omitting those items which concerned only that railway. These Rules and Regulations were appended to the Report of the House of Commons Select Committee on Railways of that year, and became the basis of all railway rule books in this country.

The punishment for disobeying the rules was severe. When an accident occurred dismissal was automatic for those responsible, although a fine might be substituted if, on enquiry, there were found to be mitigating circumstances. At the end of the Rules of 1839 under:

'Instances of Fines and Dismissal, for the Information of the Enginemen'

there are details of the following accidents and the punishments imposed:

'H.H., engineman of the Milo engine, for running carelessly against a train on Whiston incline-plane, and thereby doing considerable damage; to be suspended three days and fined ten shillings.'

'H.H., engineman, W.L. fireman, of the Eclipse engine, with luggage-train. This train followed the six o'clock blue coach-train from Manchester, on Saturday evening, and near Bury Lane ran violently against a coach-train, by which several passengers were seriously hurt, and two first-class coaches much damaged; for this act of gross carelessness, the Directors order that H.H. and W.L. be discharged.'

'J.H., engineman of the Cyclops, bank-engine, for propelling a train of goods on the level-way (on Friday morning, the 16th of June), contrary to the orders of the Directors: discharged from the service of the Company. — By order of the Directors.'

Finally:

'N.B. — Every overlooker, engineman, guard, police-man, and gateman employed in the Liverpool and Manchester Railway, shall keep a copy of these rules constantly on his person, under a penalty of a fine of five shillings. — By order of the Directors.'

In October 1830 the new engine Planet made the journey light from Edge Hill to Manchester in the hour. This engine had the wheel arrangement 2-2-0 and the cylinders were inside the frames. While this was the cause of some trouble with broken axles, until heavier and better ones were fitted, engines of this class ran far more steadily at speed than the Rocket class engines with outside cylinders and the 0-2-2 wheel arrangement. As drivers were paid on a piece work basis for each trip between Liverpool and Manchester, when the line was clear, they had a considerable inducement to emulate the Planet's feat and make the journey as quickly as possible. Drivers on the coach trains were often taking only 1 hour 10 minutes for the journey, with the stop at Newton. The Directors considered that this was too fast, and after consultation with George Stephenson, it was decided, in April 1831, that the time for the whole journey should be 1½ hours in summer and 1¾ hours in winter and an extra ½ hour for

The Planet

the journey was to be taken by the blue trains.

In December 1832 driver Robert McCree with the 10.30 a.m. blue train from Liverpool arrived in Manchester 25 minutes early. His explanation to the sub-committee was that he had a light load, very few stops and a favourable wind. A rule was then made that the blue trains should never leave Newton until one hour after leaving Liverpool or Manchester. In the same month, a complaint was received of drivers of these trains being drunk. The explanation was that the licencees of public houses adjacent to the stations served drinks to passengers when the trains stopped, and the train crews were encouraged with free drinks not to depart too expeditiously. Incidentally, two months later McCree was suspended for being drunk on a Sunday.

There were occasions when drivers were encouraged to show what could be done.

In May 1833 the Duke of Orleans* visited Liverpool, and after he had inspected the Wapping tunnel with the Mayor and Bailiff, he and his suite travelled to Manchester in a special train; this followed the 10 a.m. train, and after a stop to inspect the Sankey Viaduct, the 16 miles to Manchester were covered in half an hour, with a maximum speed of 38 m.p.h. over Chat Moss. On his arrival there the Duke gave a gratuity of £40 to be distributed among the railway staff. Normally any porter accepting a tip was liable to be dismissed. All these details were reported to the Board at its meeting on the 27th May, and it would seem that Henry Booth had travelled with the Duke, and was the source of the information.

In the summers of 1834 and 1836 a French engineer, the Comte de Pambour visited the railway, and with the support of Mr. Hardman Earle, carried out a large number of experiments on the working of the steam engine. He travelled on the engines and collected information on coke and water

---

*The Duke of Orleans was the eldest son of King Louis Philippe of France. *The Albion* reported that the Directors had made suitable preparations for the visit of the Duke, '. . . who had come for the purpose of seeing their magnificent undertaking. . . . The Prince is a handsome young man . . . and stands about five feet eight inches high. His manners are easy, unaffected and gentlemanly.' On arrival at Manchester, '. . . the Duke expressed not only his sense of politeness to the Directors, but his gratification at the mechanical wonder of the Railway.'

consumption, as well as on the effect of varying the point at which the steam supply to the cylinders was cut off. This formed part of the data given in his monumental work published in France shortly afterwards, and in English translations in 1836 and 1840 entitled *A Practical Treatise on Locomotive Engines.*

The fastest journey was on the 1st August 1834 from Manchester with a 10 wagon train, 5 of which were empty, weighing 28.2 tons; Edge Hill was reached non stop in 65½ minutes, (27¼ m.p.h.) Sutton incline being climbed without assistance. The engine was Vesta of the Planet class, built in 1832.

On the 16th July, with a 7 coach passenger train, 30.1 tons, Jupiter, another Planet class engine new in February 1831, took 72 minutes from Manchester to Edge Hill, with four minutes of stops; returning later on that day, with 8 coaches 33.1 tons, the overall time was the same but only three minutes had been spent in stops. In both trips the trains had been banked up the inclines. On the same day the 0-4-0 engine Atlas had hauled 20 wagons, 95 tons, from Edge Hill to Manchester in a nett time of 62 minutes, with 23 minutes of stops on the road, which made a gross time of 1 hour 25 minutes. The train was assisted up Whiston incline by two bank engines.

In all de Pambour made twenty-two journeys in 1834 and eight in 1836. All the latter were with one engine, the Star, with fairly heavy loads of goods wagons, and only in one instance did the average speed exceed 20 m.p.h.

In consequence of journeys being made of between 1 hour 10 minutes and 1 hour 15 minutes, in February 1835 the Directors reiterated that the journey time was to be 1½ hours and threatened drivers with fines if the time was less than 1 hour 20 minutes.

On Monday, the 20th July 1835, Lord Brougham laid the foundation stone of the new Mechanics Institute in Liverpool. He travelled from Manchester in a special train in an open carriage and he was accompanied by two of the Directors, Theodore Rathbone and Thomas Sands, and Henry Booth. According to the *Liverpool Mercury*, the journey from Manchester took only 1 hour 10 minutes. In the evening there was a dinner at the Amphitheatre in Liverpool, Lord Brougham being the principal guest. The *Liverpool Mercury* observed that he arrived an hour late when, 'The dishes had sunk to a temperature not quite agreeable to those who were nice in such matters.' After the departure of Lord Brougham at 11 o'clock, one of the speeches was by Mr. R. Rose, a coloured gentleman. There were some objections before he spoke, but there was enthusiastic applause at the end of his speech, on the subject of the great benefits of education.

By 1837 the whole track had been re-laid with heavier rails and most of the engines now had six wheels. As a result, in 1839, Rules 21 and 22 'Speed of Travelling' read as follows:

'Notice is given that during the winter months, namely, during the months of November, December, January, and February, the time for performing the trip between Edge Hill and Manchester with first-class coach-trains is one hour and a half, and with second-class trains two hours. And that during the remainder of the year the time for performing the trip with the first-class trains is one hour and a quarter, and with second-class trains one hour and three-quarters, except in foggy weather and in the dark, when the speed must be slower; the time to be taken for the trip being, in such cases, one hour and a half first-class, and two hours second-class, the same as in the winter months. And all enginemen are required to regulate the speed of their engines as accurately as practicable, according to the times specified under the several circumstances above stated.

'Engines with light loads being sometimes driven at a very great and unnecessary speed, notice is given that enginemen persisting in so injurious a practice will be fined. Engines with luggage or empty carriages should not exceed a speed of twenty miles an hour without some necessity in the case.'

In his book Whishaw describes some "Practical Railway Experiments":

'. . . undertaken for the express purpose of showing the every day work performed by different kinds of locomotive engines. . . .'

Whishaw usually travelled on the engine and most of his journeys were made in 1839. His journeys on the L&MR were all made in November, and only when the loads were heavy — 35 tons — were the times those specified for the winter months. The times with lighter loads were those for the summer months.* It would seem that there was no longer an objection to higher speeds provided the trains ran safely.

*   *   *

An article, much of which was very critical of the management of the L&MR, appeared in the October 1832 issue of the *Edinburgh Review*. Although the article was anonymous, the author was known to be Dr. Dionysus Lardner, the prominent scientist. The L&MR Board was particularly annoyed, as one of the Directors, Mr. Hardman Earle, had seen a draft of the article in July and had written to Dr. Lardner pointing out the inaccuracies it contained. The article stated that the Directors had permitted George Stephenson to import most of the staff from the North-East, and that Robert Stephenson & Company had a monopoly in the supply of engines and wagons. Further, that any suggestions for improvements were rejected and that there were objections to outside engines and wagons using the line.

The Board issued a counterblast in the form of a pamphlet and this was distributed to the Shareholders and other interested persons. The pamphlet pointed out that Mr. Earle had written to Dr. Lardner on the 16th July and that it should have been possible for the article to be corrected and revised. The misstatements were then refuted in detail. One sentence, typical of Henry Booth, said all that was needed on the subject:

'The Directors have seldom in so short a space met so many and such gross misstatements.'

The Annual Meeting in March 1832 was adjourned from Wednesday, the 28th March to Friday, the 30th March, as

---

*A detailed summary of several journeys is given in Appendix IV.

owing to the death of his father, Thomas Booth, on the previous Saturday, Henry Booth was unable to attend the meeting on the Wednesday. Although advertisements appeared in Tuesday's newspapers that the meeting was to be immediately adjourned to the Friday, several Shareholders, who had come in from the country, one of them from Kendal, not having heard that the meeting had been postponed, were very annoyed.

In January 1832 the Management Committee had arranged that the various engineers, agents and superintendents on the line should make a report giving particulars of all their staff and workmen, with details of their salaries and wages, and stating their duties and those responsible for seeing that these were correctly carried out. The Treasurer was instructed:

'. . . to prepare a detailed report on the system of management of the concern as at present carried on.'

At the meeting on Friday, Henry Booth read the account of how the railway was managed. There is no record of this statement, as in spite of a request to be allowed to be present, no representative of the Press was permitted to remain. However, in its account of the meeting, the *Liverpool Mercury* did state that:

'Henry Booth, Treasurer and Secretary, read a very long and able report of the proceedings of the Company since its commencement. Its general management and its system of superintendence, in all its various departments were explained, by which it appeared that the organization was so complete, and every essential point so well arranged, that the directors whose vigilance and attention are so highly deserving of eulogism, have all the details of this great undertaking almost daily presented to their view.'

In spite of the remarks of the *Liverpool Mercury*, it became clear in the following year that all was not well with the management and supervision of the railway. In April, Anthony Harding, an overlooker of platelayers, was dismissed when, as a result of complaints, it was discovered that he was putting in false returns of the hours worked by his staff, and. pocketing the difference between the money he received and the actual wages earned by and paid to the men.

In May, there was gossip of irregularities in the engineering workshop at Crown Street, which was managed by Mr. William Gray and his son John. There were discrepancies in the quantity of iron bought and the amount actually used, and there were rumours that in a house the company built for the Grays, staff was employed and timber used to make a more superior house than that intended by the Company. At the Board Meeting on the 17th June, Mr. Hardman Earle read out the heads of the charges against the Grays, and the meeting was adjourned until 10 a.m. the next day, Tuesday. That meeting lasted four hours and there was a further five and a half hour meeting on the Friday, fourteen witnesses being examined, and at a further meeting on Saturday, the Treasurer was asked to give details of the charges to the Grays and the meeting was adjourned until 1 p.m. on Wednesday, the 26th June. Only six Directors attended this meeting and, as the quorum was seven, the meeting was once again adjourned. The matter was finally resolved on Saturday, the 29th June. After John Gray had read a statement, it was decided that the case of misuse of timber in the house was not proved, but that as regards wrought iron, there had been substantial negligence in checking receipts and keeping details of the quantities used. It was resolved unanimously that there was not sufficient evidence to impeach the character of the Grays as zealous and well intentioned servants of the company, but John Gray was severely reprimanded for giving incorrect figures to the Sub-Committee. In view of his youth and inexperience, it was proposed to take no action against him, but the documents were to be preserved in case of future need.

As a result of these incidents, at the meeting on the 15th July, Mr. Robert Benson recommended to the Board a different arrangement of the duties and occupation of the Treasurer; the principal part of the office work to be done by clerks:

'. . . by that means the Treasurer be more at liberty to exercise a personal Superintendence & Control over the line of Railway & at the various Stations . . .'

The Board approved the plan in general, and continued the discussion a week later. The Board resolved that the Treasurer should arrange the duties of the clerks as he thought expedient:

'. . . intention of the Board that the Treasurer as general Superintendent of the various Departments of the Concern should have power to decide & act on all points arising out of the ordinary operations of the Road and touching the general business of the Company, the Sub-Committee agreed to limit their Meetings to each alternate Thursday, being the Engineers' pay day.'

The Sub-Committee had been meeting five to seven times monthly.

For some time there had been difficulties with the locomotives, some requiring boiler repairs after a very limited mileage, while others ran 20,000 miles or more without trouble. Amongst the various ideas tried out to increase the period between repairs, was the fitting of Perkins' Patent Circulator* to one engine. This appeared to have given good results, and the Directors were considering equipping most of the locomotives with this fitment. In February 1832 there was a note in the *Liverpool Times* about the engine fitted with the Circulator, from which it appeared that after 20,000 miles there had been no sign of wear in the tubes — the boiler was free from corrosion and, compared with a similar engine which had done the same work, there had been a saving of 40 tons of fuel. However, in conversation with Mr. King, the Engineer at the Gas Works, Henry Booth discovered that he had tested the Circulator and found little advantage in it. Consequently, on the 21st October, the Board decided not to contract for more of them.

---

*In locomotive boilers this consisted of a partition in the water space around the firebox; cold water went down on the outer side and as it was heated, ascended on the fire side. In stationary boilers it consisted of U-shaped pipes at the bottom of the boiler heated by the fire, with smaller diameter cylindrical pipes inside them to produce the same result.

In the report to the Shareholders in January 1833 there was a reference to the fact that locomotive expenditure had been heavier than anticipated, mentioning that it had been necessary to renew tubes and fire boxes too frequently on many of the engines. Some engines were running up to 30,000 miles with few repairs, and the Directors were confident that the problems could be solved. However, they wished the attention of scientific men to be drawn to this matter.

There was certain to be corrosion with copper or brass tubes where they were in contact with the iron boiler, unless by the use of hard water a protective layer of scale was formed on the tubes. If this became too thick the tubes would burn out, which was obviously happening fairly frequently, as drivers were provided with wooden plugs in their tool kits for isolating tubes if they burst. Although the well water at Liverpool was hard, many of the water supplies on the line came from acid peaty sources, and consequently were soft. The disappearance of these problems during the next few years was most probably due to the close attention which Henry Booth was now able to give to them.

Guards on the Second Class trains collected the fares of passengers from intermediate stations and Henry Booth reported to the Board on the 7th October, that as a result of conversations he had had with the guards, he had dismissed Mr. Roby, the principal clerk in the Manchester booking office. Mr. Roby had made a habit of keeping some of the money handed in to the guards. The Board confirmed Henry Booth's action in this matter.

Meanwhile, on the 14th October 1833, the Board decided unanimously to recommend the Shareholders to increase the salary of the Treasurer to £1,000 per annum from the £750 to which it had been raised in March 1828. At the meeting on the 23rd January 1834, the Shareholders approved the recommendation, the increase to date from the 14th October 1833.

The Railway Company's accounts, for which the Treasurer was responsible, were prepared and ready for the Directors within three weeks of the end of each half yearly period. In consequence, the date of the Annual General Meeting fixed for March in the original 1826 Act was moved forward to January in the 1837 Act. Up to the half year to June 1834 the accounts gave complete details of the running of the railway and were, therefore, of great value and encouragement to the promoters of other railways. From the end of 1834 the accounts were presented with much less detail. While this may have been due, in part, to Henry Booth's new responsibilities, the Report to the Shareholders in January 1835 stated that after four years of unreserved publicity, providing so much information to competitors was against the best interests of the company, and was not done by other railways and canal companies. *Herapath's Railway Magazine* commented in January 1836:

'We confess we think them particularly clear and explicit and we are sorry to see them giving less and less explicit detail.'

Early in 1833 there had been complaints from passengers of jostling by porters, anxious to be engaged, when trains arrived at Crown Street Station. The matter was discussed by the Sub-Committee, and it was suggested that a request be made for police to be present on the arrival of trains, as was done on the arrival of ships at the Pier Head. Charles Lawrence, the Chairman, who was a senior Magistrate, was asked to see what could be arranged. On the 12th December he reported that his colleagues would allow only one constable at Crown Street, but that: 'They recommended that one or two railway people be sworn in as special constables,' and it was ordered: 'That John Kyle, of the Crown Street Coach Yard, be sworn in accordingly.'

On Christmas morning 1833 it was discovered that the safe in the booking office at Crown Street Station, had been broken into and £57.17.6d. in cash stolen. John Kyle, who was the clerk in the booking office, usually took the cash box home and kept it in his bedroom at night, but occasionally it was locked in the safe. Kyle stated that he had been given the key of the safe by Mr. Williams, the chief clerk, at about 6 p.m. About 9 p.m. he was sitting in his own house; his wife had locked up the office for him. He then remembered that he had the key of the safe, but that he had not brought the cash box home. He stated that: 'He was much tired and had got his shoes off and thought the money would be quite safe where it was till morning.' The following morning Kyle had given the office door key to the gateman before 6 a.m. to open the door and light the fires, and at 6.30 a.m. he began to book passengers for Manchester, but he had no occasion to open the safe until the first train had departed. At 7.30 a.m. the parcel van driver told him that there was one parcel short. This had been put in the safe overnight. When the safe was opened it was discovered that the cash box and a parcel containing money were missing. Mr. Williams told the Board that the police had been called, who had examined the safe and office, but there was little hope of the robbers being apprehended. Later, Mr. Parlour, the chief of police, had examined the clerks and gate keepers, but could throw no more light on the matter.

The Board was of the opinion that John Kyle was much to be blamed for leaving the cash box in the office at night, instead of carrying it with him to his own bedroom. The Treasurer was directed to inform Kyle that should he neglect his duty again in the same way he would be dismissed from the company's service.* The Board also ordered that one of Chubb's improved locks should be put on the iron safe in the Crown Street office.

Early in 1836 there was a strike of engine drivers on the L&MR. When the railway opened, drivers and firemen were paid on a piece work basis, receiving 1/6d. and 10d. respectively for a journey between Liverpool and Manchester. Guards and policemen were paid a weekly wage of a little over £1, unskilled employees receiving about 18/- a week. As traffic increased and locomotives improved, it became possible for drivers to make several round trips per day between Liverpool and Manchester, which raised their earnings from about 30/- to £2 or more per week. The consequence was that in 1833 the Board reduced the rates for drivers and firemen to 1/3d. and 8d. a trip and in the autumn of 1835 a further reduction was proposed — drivers of passenger trains to receive 1/- and firemen 8d. a trip, and the drivers and firemen of goods trains

---

*In January 1835 John Kyle's wages were increased from 21/- to 25/- per week, and when Lime Street Station was opened in 1836, he was allowed £20 a year to compensate him for no longer having a company house. In 1840 he was dismissed for inefficiency caused by drunkenness.

1/3d. and 10d. a trip. On Sundays, when only one trip could be worked, as trains did not run in the middle of the day during the hours of church services, the drivers and firemen were to be paid 5/- and 2/6d. for the one trip. Further, in order to improve the goods services to intermediate stations, drivers and firemen were paid 1d. and ½d. for every wagon picked up during the journey. These charges were to commence on the 1st January 1836, in three months' time.

On the 29th October 1835 two drivers attended the Board Meeting and argued the case against the proposed reductions. The only concession given to them was a guaranteed minimum wage of 30/- a week. There the matter was left until the beginning of February 1836. The Directors considered that they had a good case for reducing the piece work rates, drivers being able to do three or four round trips a day. On the other hand, the building of railways in other parts of the country would increase the demand for skilled engine drivers and, not unnaturally, they felt that it was unreasonable for their wages to be reduced.

The following Minute of the Directors' Meeting on the 8th February is Henry Booth's account of what had taken place the previous week:

'The Treasurer reported that on Wednesday last there had been a Turnout amongst the Old Enginemen & Firemen. On last Monday, (February 1st.) several of the Enginemen had given verbal notice that unless the Firemen's wages were increased they would leave on Friday evening following. On Wednesday morning last the Treasurer asked John Hewitt, one of the oldest Enginemen whether he persisted in that notice & Hewitt answering that he did, the Treasurer discharged him instantly — Upon this, the other Enginemen refused to go with Trains, and some slight delay was experienced in despatching the Coach Trains — Other Enginemen however were speedily procured — some from Melling's Shed, some from Gray's Yard, and one or two New Men who had been recently engaged — Some difficulty was experienced for the first day or two in despatching the Luggage & picking up Trains — but matters were again pretty well arranged, and these

Trains were now despatched as usual — several Fitters and
Workmen from Melling's Shed and one or two Firemen
from the Manchester end had conducted themselves very
properly, and by taking the Trains promptly notwithstanding the persuasion & threats of the men who had struck, had
prevented much inconvenience to the Company — Four of
the old Enginemen who had entered into written
agreements with the Company — viz. Charles Callan, Peter
Callan, Henry Weatherburn and George Massey had been
apprehended and taken before Richard Leyland and James
Hayward Esqs. Justices of the Peace, who investigated the
circumstances of the Turnout; and the breach of Contract
being proved, committed the said offenders to Kirkdale, to
be put to hard labor for one calendar month —

'In respect of the Enginemen and Firemen who had
conducted themselves so as to merit the approbation of the
Directors, the Treasurer was instructed to present each
Engineman with a Premium of from £3 to £5 according to
circumstances and half that amount to Firemen —'

As trouble from the drivers was anticipated, steps must have
been taken to have replacement drivers available. That the
new drivers were not as skilled as the regular drivers came out
in the half yearly Report on the 27th July 1836.

'Amongst items of expenditure, those for Locomotive
Power & Coach and Wagon disbursements have been
increased, in this half year, by various accidents occasioning
the breakage of engines, wagons and coaches; one of the
consequences of a general strike on the part of the
locomotive engineers.'

A somewhat different account of the strike was given by the
Manchester Guardian and quoted by *The Albion* on the 8th
February, which confirms the view that steps were being taken
to train new drivers. Turnouts were a frequent item of news in
the Manchester area, but the strike was ignored by the
majority of Liverpool newspapers. The paragraph in *The
Albion* read:

Henry Booth

Thomas Booth jun.
(Painting in possession of Mr. C.E. Booth)

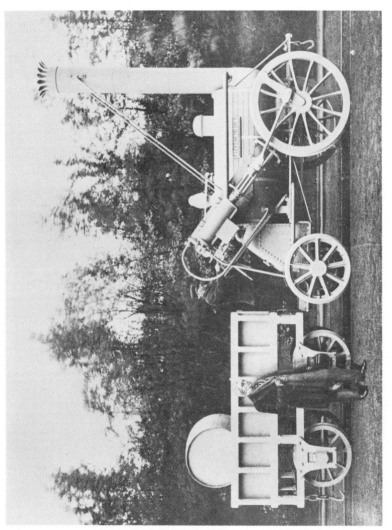

The Rocket — replica built at the Crewe Works in 1879

Birthplace in Rodney Street – the plaque is visible to the left of the doors

Residence – Eastbourne in Princes Park

Ancient Chapel — south-east end and graveyard

Ancient Chapel — south-west side

Rainhill today looking east – scene of trials

Rainhill today looking west showing skew bridge

Silver tray presented to Henry Booth

Statue of Henry Booth in St. Georges Hall, Liverpool
(By courtesy of the *Daily Post*)

'Turn Out of Engine Men — The Directors were exposed to some inconvenience from a Turn Out of Engine Drivers. The Directors being anxious to increase the number of drivers and having men of more mechanical skill taught to manage engines, gave directions that two or three mechanics from their workshops should go with Drivers as Firemen. The Drivers were apprehensive and objected as diminishing their importance. Two positively refused to start with new assistants. They were discharged on the spot, and all the Drivers and some Firemen left their employment after completion of their first trips. Consequently there was considerable irregularity in departures and more in arrivals of trains on that day. The Directors resolved to persevere, and filled the places of Turn Outs from amongst mechanics, whose previous knowledge of the construction of engines very soon enabled them to overcome every difficulty in their new vocation. The working has now resumed accustomed regularity. The Turn Outs earned 40/- per week.'

A week later, on the 13th February, the *Liverpool Chronicle* reported:

'Three or four Railway Engineers employed by the Railway have been sent to study practical mechanics on the rotatory machine, commonly called the treadmill, for having left their work contrary to the terms of their several employments.'

At the meeting of the Directors on the 22nd February, a letter was read from the Chaplain at Kirkdale Prison, petitioning that the four drivers should be relieved from the severe labour on the treadmill. While the Directors were disposed to mitigate the penalty, it had become a matter for the magistrates. Fortunately, Mr. W.W. Currie, one of the Marquis of Stafford's Directors, was then Mayor and Chief Magistrate, and it was arranged that he would see what could be done for the men.

The difficulties experienced as a result of the strike convinced Henry Booth that steps should be taken to prevent

J

the danger of such stoppages by key staff without adequate notice.

Shortly after the formation of the L&NWR there was a strike of engine drivers on the Southern Division. It caused great inconvenience and one serious accident. In January 1850, when there was a possibility of a further strike, Henry Booth, at a meeting of the Crewe Locomotive Committee, urged the expediency of consideration being given to:

> 'Some legislative sanction for mutual and reciprocal engagements (subject to agreed notice) between Railway Companies and Enginemen as may prevent the difficulties and risks consequent on a sudden and general strike amongst Enginemen on any Railway.'

A recommendation to this effect was sent to the General Locomotive Committee in London to pass on to the L&NWR Board. The Board was preoccupied with other matters and no action was taken when the report of the General Locomotive Committee received attention on the 9th March, after two adjournments of the February meeting.

The prison treadmill

Chapter VIII

Henry Booth took out several patents during the next few years. These were the result of his close contact with the day to day working of the railway.

Oil was used to lubricate the bearings of the wagons and coaches and this dripped out and had to be constantly renewed. Henry Booth experimented with mixtures of tallow and palm oil, emulsified by heating with washing soda to just under boiling point with vigorous stirring, so that a butter like grease was produced which could be put in axle boxes of railway vehicles. It melted after the axle ran hot, forming a lubricating film on the heated surface, and an axle box of suitable size only required re-filling once a week. Greases based on this formula were regularly used on railway vehicles until the advent of roller bearings.*

The grease was used by the L&MR, but there is no information as to whether Henry Booth received any payment in this connection. On the other hand, on the 13th June 1839, the London & Birmingham Railway Board resolved:

'To offer £100 to Mr. Booth for the licence to use his patent grease.'

Mr. Baxendale, the outdoor Superintendent was instructed to negotiate, but it appears to have been Mr. R. Creed, the

*Patent No. 6814 — 14/4/1835.

Secretary, who sent the offer. Henry Booth replied to it on the 22nd June 1839:

> 'I am obliged by your letter of the 20th and by your kind feeling on my behalf in this little matter between your redoubtable Company and myself. My opinion is not altered; but that is not the question. I will not have a contest with the London & Birm^m.R.W.
>
> 'Please say to the Board that you have authority to conclude the arrangement on their own terms and excuse the trouble —'

In evidence before the House of Commons Committee on railways in April 1841, Henry Booth stated that for the first two years the railway was operating, there were no spring buffers in use on the L&MR's passenger rolling stock. In the third edition — 1838 — of Nicholas Wood's book on railroads there is a drawing showing spring buffers being used in combination with spring drawgear, which had been developed in the company's workshop.* The replica L&MR coaches at the National Railway Museum at York have a different type of spring buffer based on the patent — No. 6781 - 4/3/1835 — taken out by Mr. T.F. Bergin, Engineer of the Dublin & Kingstown Railway. In Bergin's patent there is only one central buffer, while the L&MR coaches have two, one on each side. Mr. Bergin had corresponded with the L&MR on several subjects, and at the Board Meeting on the 23rd November 1835 Henry Booth had produced copies of the *Mechanic's Magazine* with details of Bergin's patent.

A few years later various patents were taken out for spring buffers with the spring inside the actual buffer, and these replaced the more complicated types.

The replica carriages at the National Railway Museum are fitted with single screw couplings. In Henry Booth's patent, No. 6989 - 8/3/1836 — the coupling had a double screw with opposite threads on each side of the lever used to reduce the

---

*In the patent specification the previous method of coupling is shown as a chain of 11 links between two hooks.

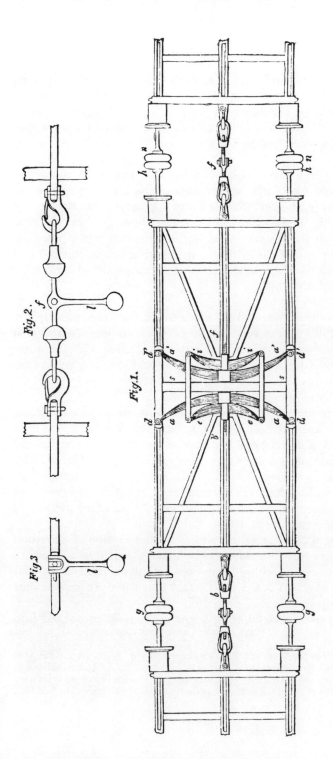

Fig.2. *f*

l

Fig.3

l

Fig.1.

h n

f

d' a' i i a' d'

s *f* *s*

d a e b e a d

b

g

b

g

h n

Booth's patent coupling

length of the coupling.* The result was that turning the lever clockwise the coupling was tightened, while turning it anti-clockwise increased the length. To quote Robert Smiles, the combination of spring buffers and springs on the draw bars of the carriages resulted in:

'. . . the prevention of discomfort and suffering, of the jars and jolts, and pitching about, by the coupling screws and spring buffers invented and applied by Mr. Booth. . . . upon the Liverpool and Manchester line. . . . the practical value of the coupling and buffing apparatus in preventing violent pulsations in trains, in securing steady starting and smooth running, and abating tear and wear of both road and rolling stock.'

On the 13th March 1837 the L&MR Directors paid Henry Booth 150 guineas for the use of his coupling. In the first instance it was used only on First Class coaches and it was not liked by the drivers, as the whole train had to be started as one, rather than starting each carriage separately, due to the slack in the chains previously used.

The double screw coupling was first used on the Grand Junction and London & Birmingham Railways and was then gradually adopted by all railways in Great Britain and Ireland and in Europe and elsewhere. It is still in use on older vehicles here and in Europe. In Europe, owing to the number of railway authorities and the time taken to reach an agreement on a replacement, it only ceased to be the standard method of coupling trains in the 1970s.

In patent No. 6989 there was also a description of a method of stopping steam locomotives by placing a slide or damper to close the exhaust pipe from the cylinders. This somewhat illogical idea was based on the fact that when steam was shut off to stop the engine, a vacuum was created in the cylinders and abrasive particles of unburnt coke could be sucked into

---

*G.P. Neele in his *Notes of a Railway Superintendent's Life*, states that Abel Turton, once Stationmaster at Parkside, told him that he had suggested to Henry Booth the desirability of having a screw shackle or coupling between the carriages to bring the buffers together, and that the suggestion had been adopted.

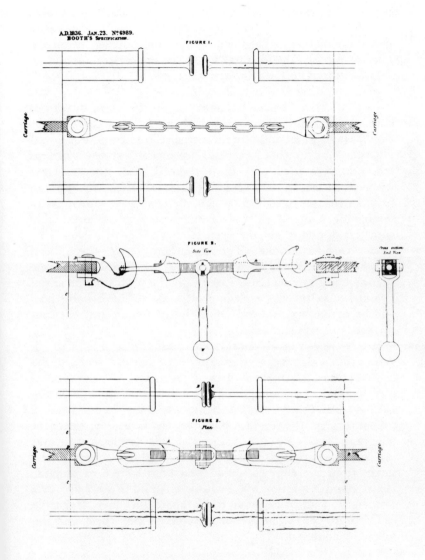

FIGURE 1.

Carriage

Carriage

FIGURE 2.
Side View

Cross section
End View

FIGURE 3.
Plan

Carriage

Carriage

Booth's patent coupling

the cylinders causing damage. Owing to the fact that no brakes were fitted to engines, but only to the tenders, it was usual to stop them by leaving the throttle open and putting the engine in reverse gear. The idea was not taken up as later a steam jet (blower) direct to the chimney was used.

Henry Booth's next patent — No. 7335 - 4/10/1837 — was for a locomotive furnace to enable coal to be burnt instead of coke. As coal cost about a third of the price of coke, its use would result in a considerable saving in fuel costs, but it was essential that the coal burnt did not produce smoke. Various methods were tried out on the L&MR and other railways without success. In Henry Booth's patent there was a hopper in front of the fire box from which the coal was pushed on to sloping fire-bars. With coal of mixed sizes it was impossible with this device to get the even feed required if it was to be burnt without smoke. The invention would have been successful if there had been graded coal, which did not become available until much later. Eventually the problem was solved by putting a fire brick arch in the fire box. This became hot, and by arranging to direct the unburnt smoke under its hot surface, this was consumed.

Henry Booth also considered taking out a patent in connection with another matter in which he was interested; the construction of tunnels used by locomotives. All the tunnels were worked by stationary engines and a rope haulage on the L&MR, but other railways being built involved having a tunnel through the top of a pass over the hills. The electrical telegraph was only in the process of development, and breakdowns in tunnels with little or no visibility, owing to the steam from the engines, could well be a source of danger. Henry Booth's solution was a simple one and is described in a contribution which he made to *Herapath's Railway Magazine* in February 1837. The Editor introduced the article with the following comment:

'The following communication will be read with great interest as coming from a gentleman of well known experience and sound judgement in railway matters. If any theory can render tunnels tolerable, we are satisfied Mr. Booth's will.'

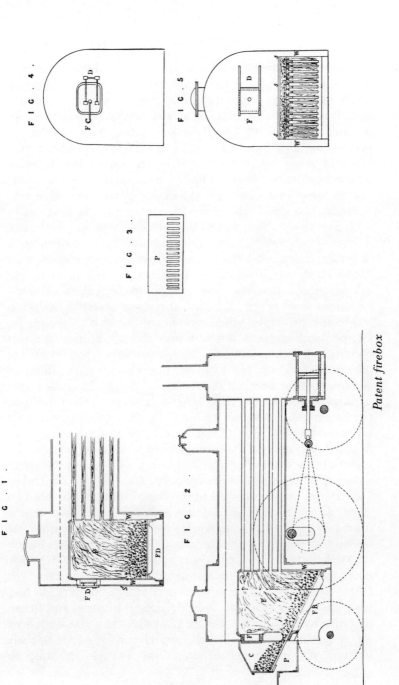

Patent firebox

The article pointed out that in tunnels the rails were likely to be moist, so that there would be reduced adhesion; slipping would increase the amount of exhaust steam and this would fill the tunnel. When two engines passed the noise would be like continuous musketry with more steam and smoke in proportion, and matters would be made worse if a boiler tube burst or some other fault developed. To surmount these problems, Henry Booth proposed constructing two tunnels, one for use in each direction. If a tunnel passed through a hill, it would be a simple matter to have a descending gradient in each direction of 10 or 12 feet per mile resulting in a difference of level of only 5 or 6 feet between the two lines at each end of a mile long tunnel. As a result there would be much less steam in each tunnel, and it would not take long for this to clear. He acknowledged that the solution would be easier in some situations than others, but that there was scarcely any place where the principle would not be of advantage. Actually, Henry Booth did not proceed with the application for this patent; ten years later the development of the electrical telegraph resulted in it being possible to have lines of communication between the two ends of tunnels.

As mentioned, ropes were used for haulage in the tunnels at the Liverpool end of the railway. In 1832 two patents were taken out by a Mr. J.H. Kyan for preserving rope and timber in damp conditions. The process used was to impregnate the material in a bath of corrosive sublimate (Mercuric Chloride — a highly poisonous Mercury Salt). On the 3rd September 1834 Henry Booth reported to the Board that he had put two pieces of white rope into a damp hole for three months; one untreated piece and the other treated with Kyan's solution. At the end of three months the untreated rope was very much decayed and the treated piece apparently sound. He now proposed to test the ropes for tensile strength. On the 17th November he made a further report on the matter. He had tested two ropes by suspending weights from them and found that the Kyanized rope was 25% weaker than the untreated piece. As the ropes in use in the tunnels lost only 25% of their strength after prolonged service, there was no advantage in using the process, which was expensive.*

However, the process was used on the L&MR and other railways for treating larch sleepers, which proved to be superior to the stone blocks originally used on the railways. It is not known whether the health of the staff handling the Kyanized timber was affected. The *Mechanic's Magazine* reported in 1838 that the giraffes in the Zoological Gardens in Regent's Park had a sickly appearance, apparently due to licking Kyanized fencing. They lacked sprightliness and lustre in the eyes compared with giraffes in a Surrey zoo. In 1839 the *Railway Magazine* stated that railways: '. . . have started using a material they call Kreosote,' and this soon replaced the Kyan solution.

In 1836 a Commission was set up to make recommendations about railways in Ireland and on the 28th November the L&MR Board received a request from the Secretary to the Commission for information on the working of the railway. The Treasurer was instructed to prepare a draft reply, and this was approved at the next Board Meeting. The reply to the Commission was not published, but a copy is preserved in the Goldsmiths Library of London University.** The Commissioners followed the recommendations, which produced a more logical railway system than in the British Isles. The reply pointed out that more capital expenditure was still required over the amount shown in the accounts, which were attached to the letter, and continued:

'. . . the traffic on the Liverpool and Manchester Railway yields a very large gross income, amounting to about £200,000 per annum, or nearly £7,000 per mile; and experience abundantly proves that a large traffic can be conducted far more economically than a small one. And hence it becomes obvious, that though one Railway, with a given traffic, yield a nett income of ten per cent, it by no means follows that the same traffic divided between two Railways would yield to each a nett income of five per cent.'

*Mercuric Chloride is hydrolysed in solution and, in consequence, reacts as an acid and this weakens any cellulose material.
**In the catalogue the author is given as Henry Booth and the signature on the letter is that of Henry Booth.

Henry Booth had drawn attention to a fact which has only been appreciated in the last twenty years of operating railways; that it is essential for railways to have a large traffic if they are to be run economically.

'. . . the Liverpool and Manchester Railway, in reference to the formation of the road, and to all its moving machinery, is yet far from being completed. From the opening of the Railway to the present time, and more especially for the last twelve or eighteen months, we have been in a state of transition, passing from the defective and imperfect in form and construction, to more improved forms, and especially to increased strength, in engines, coaches, and waggons. In the original formation of the road, imperfect rails, insufficient sleepers, and inadequate draining have been, and still are, the cause of heavy and constant expenditure. Gradually these defects are in course of being remedied; but time and money are indispensable in this process, and the work of transition from wrong to right is yet far from being accomplished. Further time will be needed, and further sums must be expended. New Railways will have a great advantage in this respect. In the formation of the road, in the mechanics of the engines, in the construction of the carriages, in every thing which constitutes the working of a Railway, they will start at a point which we have not yet reached, or only in solitary instances. Under such circumstances, and with an improved system from the commencement, it seems reasonable to anticipate that with an equal traffic, their comparative disbursements will be less; but as to how much less, we have literally no experience to guide us.

'With reference to the broader question of the principle and system on which Railways should be established in a new country, I will trespass on your time with a very few observations.

'Some preliminary points seem necessary to be settled at the outset. Are the Railways in Ireland to be considered in the light of mercantile speculations, not to be undertaken except with the prospect of a remunerating profit or must we regard them as great and beneficial works, to be undertaken for the improvement of the country, and to be sustained by the hand of Government, where private means are insufficient? It is evident that on this latter principle, the Commissioners might suggest the construction of great lines of Railway, which, on the former principle they would hardly take upon themselves the responsibility to recommend. Under any circumstances, however, it seems desirable to consider pretty closely what it is that is required.

'A Railway is a very indefinite object; it is the kind of Railway that must, in the first place, be determined. England with her commerce, her manufactures, and her wealth, already aims at a scale of perfection far beyond any thing hitherto attained. A speed of thirty miles an hour, with the luxury of the smoothest motion which springs and cushions can afford, we have at present. But by many this is still the aim; and it is evident that in a large class of minds improvement is anticipated in speed of conveyance rather than in cheapness of conveyance. Probably this expectation should be modified with reference to Ireland; and that cheapness and facility of intercommunication should be the main object, rather than the attainment of an extreme speed. On the settlement of this point will depend the nature of the gradients that are to be adopted, and also very considerably the cost of the undertaking.

'Much discussion has taken place on this side of the Channel, as to the desirableness of an increased width of way; and the Commissioners, no doubt, are aware that the "Great Western" Railway Company have adopted the recommendation of their engineer, and are about to construct their road seven feet wide between the rails. The plea for this extraordinary departure from the width of way hitherto in practice, is, that by the steadiness which will result to the engine and carriages from a much wider base, they will be able to use wheels of larger diameter, and thereby attain a much higher speed, with a reduced ratio of friction. To a certain extent these objects will be gained, though at a considerably increased cost. The dead weight of the engine and carriages, in proportion to the profitable load, will be much greater than with the ordinary width;

and the cost of all sorts of vehicles will be much higher; add to which there will be more difficulty in passing round curves, and consequently in moving from one line of way to another, and the carriages will be more cumbrous to arrange at the different stations. The present width of way I consider hardly sufficient; but an addition of six inches would afford ample means of improving the arrangement and proportions of the machinery, as well as of giving increased steadiness, and the capability of increased velocity to the engine and carriages.'

The gauge of 5′3″ adopted in Ireland was 6½″ more than the English gauge and this is also the gauge in Victoria and South Australia, India and the San Paulo Railway in Brazil. In Russia, Spain, Portugal and the Argentine the gauge is 5′6″; in Russia and Spain for security reasons, to be different from neighbouring countries.

'In devising a system of Railways for a new country, it will be very important to attend to unity of design and plan, with a view, hereafter, to unity of management and control. Great trunks, main lines from capital to capital, or from one principal town to another, afford the best scope for the peculiar advantages of Railways; the accommodation of smaller and intermediate places must be held subservient to the arrangements on the main line. Small sacrifices of time and distance on the part of intermediate places, in order to effect a junction convenient to the main line, are, when rightly considered, no sacrifices at all; for ultimately, whatever tends to the ensuring of order and despatch along the main line must be generally beneficial to the intermediate places . . . .'

'But perhaps the most important point to which the consideration of the Commissioners will immediately be turned, is the economical application of the funds placed at their disposal, so that the greatest possible benefit may be derived from a certain stipulated expenditure; and the most obvious and simple rule for the attainment of this end seems to be, to take care not to construct two main lines of Railway where one will suffice. So self-evident, indeed, and so much in the nature of a truism, is this proposition, that I should not have ventured to allude to it, if the very reverse of this rule did not seem to prevail on this side of the Channel; for in England, no sooner is a certain district of country provided with a Railway, than rival lines are projected before the first line is in operation, and before it has been at all proved, not that the first line is not sufficient, but that it is not much more than sufficient for the exigencies of the country through which it passes. With the most chivalrous disregard of consequences, and the most disinterested neglect of all sober and rational calculation, the projectors of Railways, in this country, are content to discuss the merits of sections and gradients; and forgetting that no line can be a good one, where no Railway is required . . . and as yet we have no evidence of any one controlling mind, feeling the importance of taking a broad view of the whole question, and of estimating beforehand what effect these innumerable crude and disjointed, but in the aggregate, stupendous, projects, will produce on the state of trade, on the stability of credit, and consequently on the general prosperity and well-being of the nation. What course Ministers will take in these extraordinary circumstances, whether they will leave the nation to its madness, or exercise a timely control to prevent or to limit this threatened waste of the national resources, a little time will show. In Ireland the position of things is different; but even there, the contemplation of what is passing in England may not be without its lesson; for in all countries, and under all circumstances, it is an object worthy of a statesman to prevent the reckless waste of the national means, and to give a right direction to the public expenditure.'

The L&MR was the scene of a number of scientific experiments carried out mainly at the Whiston incline between Huyton and Rainhill. As has been mentioned earlier, experiments were made there in 1830 on the resistance of various types of wagons. In 1837, Mr. Nicholas Wood and Professor Lardner carried out a number of experiments as to wind resistance. Henry Booth's interest in these last experiments was shown when on Tuesday, the 12th February 1839, he read the

presidential address at the inaugural meeting of the Liverpool
Polytechnic Society. His address was entitled 'Some Observations of the Force of the Wind and the Resistance of the Air'.
Nicholas Wood's experiments were to ascertain the resistance
of the air against a train of four First Class railway carriages,
the front of the first carriage presenting a flat surface of about
30 sq.ft. Small scale experiments had shown that the force of
the wind varied with the square of the velocity. To quote from
the address:

> 'But besides the resistance against the front of the first
> carriage, there would be resistance along the sides and tops
> of the carriages, and underneath them; also by the axles,
> and by the peripheries and spokes of the wheels. The form
> of the hindmost end of the last coach (that of a square flat
> surface of the same dimensions as the front end of the first
> coach), would also tend to increase considerably the
> resistance offered by the air to a train of carriages at a high
> velocity. This negative resistance (if I may so call it),
> occasioned by the flat end of the last carriage, is to be
> attributed to the disturbance of the equilibrium of the
> atmospheric pressure. If the carriages are moved through
> the air at a very high velocity, a partial vacuum is created in
> the rear of the last coach, before the atmosphere has time to
> close in behind; and this partial vacuum in the rear will
> increase the resistance in front. The same principle operates
> more obviously, in the case of a vessel moving through
> water. . . . In addition, therefore, to the resistance which a
> train of carriages meets with in front, when forced through
> the air (and which is similar to the force of the wind upon
> opposing surfaces, at similar velocities), there is the
> resistance arising from the disturbance of the equilibrium of
> the pneumatic pressure, occasioned by the square flat form
> of the carriages, behind, — a resistance which I believe has
> not yet been noticed by writers on this subject.'

*   *   *

Lime Street Station had been opened in August 1836. The
Board Room and offices were moved there from the various

places in which they had been housed. The Crown Street Station became a coal depot and the workshops there were gradually extended. At Manchester the station was improved; the station was at a high level after the line crossed the Irwell, and the space below was used to provide new stables. There had been talk of extending the line further into the centre of the town, but with the prospective opening of the Manchester & Leeds (later Lancashire & Yorkshire) Railway, a joint station with that company was desirable. As trade was depressed, action was deferred until it was possible for the expenditure to produce profits. This attitude was one which Henry Booth adopted in all his reports to the L&NWR Board in 1848-49; that large capital expenditure on railways should not be incurred until there was a certainty of eventual profit.

By 1837 the transition from 'the defective and imperfect in form and construction, to more improved forms' was beginning to bear fruit. In the report to the proprietors in July of that year, it was mentioned that:

'. . . the Grand Junction Railway has been opened, for the conveyance of PASSENGERS between Liverpool and Manchester, and Birmingham.* Proprietors are aware that the Engines and Carriages of the Grand Junction Company pass along the Liverpool and Manchester Line, as far as Warrington Junction. A considerable accession of revenue may be expected from this source.'

After referring to the relaying of the track with heavier rails, it continued:

'In their last report, the Directors informed the proprietors, that in the management of the Railway, their primary object had been to provide that full satisfaction to the Public, which affords in its turn, the surest basis for the permanent prosperity of the Railway. In the Half-year just closed the Coaching Department has been conducted in a manner superior to what they had previously been able to accomplish. There have been more Departures in the day,

*On the 4th July 1837.

K

and the Trips have been performed with greater expedition, and with more uniform punctuality; add to which, Passengers at the Liverpool End are brought by the New Tunnel to the middle of the Town, instead of being set down in Crown Street, a mile and a-half from the centre of business. The means employed to attain this End have been principally a larger and superior class of Locomotive Engine, and very complete Machinery for working the New Tunnel.

The accounts for the second half of 1837 showed a small increase in profits. A fall in receipts of £5,200 was more than compensated for by a reduction of £6,700 in expenses. Mr. Herapath, the proprietor, commented in the *Railway Magazine*:

'It is, however, but justice to observe, that all this credit is not due to the Directors alone; their very excellent Treasurer and Secretary, Mr. Henry Booth, to whom the concern is so deeply indebted for its past and present prosperity, is entitled to a very large share of it, as every one who knows anything of this Railway must admit.'

On the 25th July 1838 at the half-yearly meeting, the Treasurer's salary was increased from £1,000 to £1,500 per annum. Mr. Herapath wrote:

'If ever any man deserved such a mark of approbation, we are sure we speak the sentiments of the whole railway world when we say, that that man is Henry Booth.'

Trade was still depressed, but the tolls paid by the GJR helped to maintain receipts, and in the winter of 1837-38 there was a severe frost resulting in canal transport being unavailable, so that railway receipts continued to increase. However, as the depression in trade continued in 1839 and 1840, the Board had not taken any firm decision on the Manchester extension.*

*A decision was reached regarding the new station at Manchester in 1842 and it was opened in 1844.

In July 1840 Mr. Robert Gill, a Director of the Manchester
& Leeds Railway attended the General Meeting of the L&MR
Company. After the meeting he sent a printed circular letter to
the newspapers and others in which he said that after arriving
from Manchester he reached the room in which the meeting
was being held at three minutes past one, the meeting being
advertised for 1 p.m. Mr. Gill stated that he represented large
proprietors in Manchester and London who wanted action to
effect the connection needed with the Manchester & Leeds
Railway. He claimed that the canal interests represented by
Mr. Loch for the Duke of Sutherland, were anxious to stop
competition with the canals and that the Directors were
subservient to these interests. He stated that he had seen the
Chairman and Actuary [Treasurer] a week before the meeting
and offered to attend a Board Meeting. When he arrived the
Chairman was dissolving the meeting, although few Shareholders had arrived. His proposition was objected to by Mr.
Cropper [J. Cropper Junior] who stated that it should have
gone through the Board and attempted to deny that the Board
knew anything about it. The few Shareholders present then
encouraged the Chairman to dissolve the meeting, and this was
done at 1.11 p.m. The circular letter then continued with Mr.
Gill's proposition, which he had sent in a letter to the
Chairman of the L&MR:

'The importance of a Junction with the great lines
north-east of Manchester having been already admitted, by
a successful application to Parliament, during the last
session, I am deputed by parties largely interested in
carrying out the powers so granted that should the
unwillingness on the part of the Board of Directors of the
Liverpool and Manchester Railroad still exist, to enter into
an engagement for renting the whole property of the
Company, paying the proprietors a larger dividend than
they have hitherto received — viz. ten per cent., the
maximum allowed by their act of incorporation —
contingent on the formation of the Junction with the
Manchester and Leeds Line at Hunt's Bank, Manchester —
for the outlay of which they will allow an interest-charge of
five per cent. per annum, and ample security will be

provided whenever required.'

There then followed a number of wild assertions about the reasons for the L&MR not having taken any action.

This resulted in the L&MR Board issuing a printed 'Postscript' to the half-yearly report of 29th July 1840, and in the next issue of *Herapath's Railway Magazine* and other papers there was a letter from Henry Booth reading:

'A brief statement of the facts in opposition to the extraordinary specimen of misrepresentation which Mr. Robert Gill has thought proper to publish to the world — The Meeting did not begin until 1.05 p.m., the ordinary routine. The Clerk read the notice of the Meeting and the Treasurer read the Report and Statement of accounts, the annual disbursements and capital expenditure, and details of shares on which dividends were to be paid. The report was approved, being moved and seconded by two proprietors and carried by a show of hands.

'The five per cent dividend was moved and seconded and carried (hardly needed as it was in the report). The Chairman stated that he or the Treasurer would answer any questions; there was a pause. A proprietor from Manchester moved the thanks of the Meeting to the Chairman, the Shareholders began to depart and then Mr. Gill stepped forward saying that he had a proposition being copied downstairs, but which proposition, as mentioned previously, the Shareholders declined to receive.'

The Postscript, which was sent to all Shareholders and to the Press, opened with the same paragraph as the letter and continued:

'. . . but the Directors did not expect that any Proprietor of their concern would send forth to the Public such a gross misrepresentation of the facts of the case, accompanied by the most calumnious charges against themselves, and especially against the Chairman of the Meeting.'

After giving the time-table of the meeting, the Postscript

continued:

> 'Mr. Gill goes on to say that the reason, "Why such unusual haste was exercised, on this occasion, will be best explained by the Chairman; that he must be allowed to express his own opinion, that there were reasons for such haste, and such haste was not creditable to the parties who promoted it."
>
> 'The insinuation is as much without foundation as the fact. The proceedings were conducted with the customary forms, and in the usual routine.'

As mentioned earlier, Mr. Gill had claimed that the L&MR Board was subservient to the canal interests, and in a letter to the *Liverpool Chronicle* of the 1st August had complained about the insufficiency of the tolls charged to the GJR for the use of the line. After dealing with these matters, the Postscript ended:

> 'The Leeds Junction is the only serious question Mr. Gill is labouring to force on the Proprietors of the Liverpool and Manchester company . . . the outlay to be incurred . . . requiring the most deliberate consideration: and the Proprietors will now be aware, that the difficulty imposed on the Directors has not been lightened by their having been called upon to discuss these points with the manager of the Manchester and Leeds Railway.
>
> Railway Office, Liverpool, 3rd August 1840.'

* * *

When George Stephenson ceased to be the Engineer and became a Consultant to the company, his principal assistant John Dixon was promoted to Engineer; he was a civil engineer and his major responsibility was the maintenance of the track, and the running of the trains. The consequence was that the two workshops in Liverpool, where most of the repairs to locomotives, carriages and wagons were carried out, became increasingly the domain of the foremen, William Gray and his son John at Crown Street and John Melling at Edge Hill. John

Melling and John Gray took out patents on ideas they had for
the improvement of the locomotives, but when some of their
inventions were tried out by the railway they did not prove
successful.* In December 1833 Mr. John Cropper recommended a young man, Mr. Edward Woods, to the Board, and
he was made Assistant Engineer at Manchester. When Mr.
Dixon left in the autumn of 1836, Woods was promoted to be
Engineer, but remaining at Manchester.

In November 1839 the Board agreed to a suggestion by
Henry Booth that he should put forward a plan to reorganize
the engineering workshops. The new scheme was for a Chief
Engineer to be appointed, who would be in complete charge of
all the workshops, with a Superintendent under him. At the
beginning of December the plan was approved and the
Treasurer was instructed to carry it out and to report progress
from time to time. Mr. Woods was made Chief Engineer and
put in charge of all the workshops, as well as continuing his
previous duties. He was to work under the advice and control
of the Treasurer, and the Directors were expecting a
diminution of expenses as a result of this appointment. At the
end of December the Treasurer reported that he had given
three months' notice to Mr. Melling and Mr. William Gray of
Liverpool and Mr. Fyfe of Manchester.**

On the 27th January 1840 the Treasurer reported to the

---

*Melling's Patent, No. 7410 - 26/7/1837, lists six different inventions. The
first, a coupling wheel, to avoid the use of coupling rods on locomotives. In the
drawing a third wheel held in place against the driving wheel by steam
pressure causes the front carrying wheel to rotate, but as the front wheel is
smaller than the driving wheel, it did not work. Ahrons states that it was
fitted to the locomotive Arrow which was completed in May 1837. It was
mentioned in de Pambour's treatise — page 34, and was tried 60 years later by
Mr. F.W. Webb on the L&NWR, but with wheels of the same diameter. The
second was to use two wheels in a similar manner; as they ran in opposite
directions a braking effect was produced. The third, a simpler method for
working the valves of the engine; it was tested by the railway in October 1837.
The fourth was to heat the feed water for the boiler by letting the ashes fall
into a tank under the firebox, and to let the steam from the safety valve also go
into it, so that the boiler feed would be near the boiling point. The fifth, to use
a steam jet 'for the purpose of cleansing the rails from snow, grease, or sand,
while the engine is travelling thereon, . . .' The sixth was a modification of the
first, using the wheel driven by the piston to drive two smaller wheels of the
same size, the driving wheel being two inches clear of the rails.
**Mr. John Gray had already left the company.

The Ostrich

Board that he had appointed Mr. John Dewrance, a foreman with the Manchester firm of engine builders, Peel Williams, to take charge of the workshops at a salary of £250 per annum and the free tenancy of the house occupied by Mr. Melling; and that Mr. Woods would be moving to Liverpool on the 2nd March. Having the two principal officers in daily contact with Henry Booth resulted in big improvements in the performance of the locomotives. As a first step, in April, drivers were given a bonus for economizing in the use of coke, so that consumption fell from 49 to 40 lbs per mile. During 1840 Dewrance carried out a large number of tests on how to set the valves and the best dimensions to get the most economical use of the steam, and as a result coke consumption was nearly halved.

In the *Railway Magazine* of the 27th November 1841, Mr. Herapath reported on this work. Mr. Dewrance was giving the valves greater lap — so using the steam more expansively — and had increased the blast pipe diameter from $2^5/8''$ to $4^3/8''$, resulting in a 'sweeter draught, which did not tear the fire to pieces'. The engines Rokeby and Roderic, which had been burning 42.9 and 40.8 lbs of coke per mile respectively in March 1840, were burning only 17.1 and 17.5 lbs in April 1841. The steam ports and pipes in the engines were large to facilitate the passage of steam, a point which later designers sometimes overlooked with bad results. Finally, over the last twelve months there had been 'only two detentions . . . from derangements of engines, no crank axle breakages or derailments.'*

In 1841 all the new engines, incorporating the various improvements, were being built in the company's workshops, and the coke consumption on these engines was as little as 15 lbs per mile. These engines were given the names of birds and twenty-eight passenger engines of the 2-2-2 wheel arrangement and eight goods engines 2-4-0's were built. In April 1843, Mr. Herapath reported in the *Railway Magazine*, that in the week ending the 29th July 1842, coke consumption on 139 passenger trips between Liverpool and Manchester had

*Mr. Herapath in a conversation with 'Mr. Booth and Mr. Woods' on a subject which he had been writing about in the *Railway Magazine*, found that they preferred six wheeled to four wheeled engines, but considered there was no substantial difference with a good engine and a good road.

averaged 14½ lbs per mile, and on 62 goods trips the average was 16¾ lbs.

Over the next four years, when receipts were tending to fall owing to the depression in trade, locomotive expenses decreased so much that in all but one half year the profit was sufficient to pay the usual 5% dividend. The effectiveness of the reorganization is shown by the graph in Appendix V.

* * *

Henry Booth had given evidence in June 1832 to the Committee of the House of Lords dealing with the London & Birmingham Railway Bill. On that occasion his object was to show the benefits which had arisen from the opening of the L&MR. On the 19th March 1841 he gave evidence to the House of Commons Select Committee on Railways, and dealt with, and was questioned on, the technical side of railway management. He stated that he was the General Manager of the railway.

The Committee was concerned with the desirability of railways running to exact time tables, and trains leaving at not less than 15 minute intervals. Henry Booth was against both ideas. On the L&MR with a 30 mile journey of eighteen stops, it was not possible to fix an exact time of departure for every intermediate stop, and there were often extra goods trains being run for some special traffic with little notice. He had no use for the suggestion of a 15 minute interval system. On the L&MR line, with a considerable passenger and goods traffic, it was essential to run the trains as close together as possible, always arranging for the coach trains to depart first, to be followed by the stopping and goods trains. With this arrangement the following train left when the preceding train had travelled half a mile, and the orders were that this interval should always be maintained. Safety on railways resulted from drivers being alert at all times, and the good accident record on the L&MR proved that this was the correct policy. He considered unsatisfactory the suggestion that a red signal should be exhibited for ten minutes after a train left the station and a green signal for the next five minutes. On the L&MR this would result in drivers frequently passing red signals at

every station and so no longer regarding it in all cases as a
signal to stop.

*   *   *

In December 1844 a special meeting of the Shareholders
approved the amalgamation of the Liverpool & Manchester
Railway with the North Union,* Grand Junction, Kenyon &
Leigh and Bolton & Leigh Railways; the GJR absorbing the
other lines. The Act confirming this was passed in September
1845. Henry Booth was appointed Secretary of the GJR, and in
November there was a meeting of Shareholders to sanction the
further amalgamation of that railway with the London &
Birmingham.

It was generally recognized that the amalgamations marked
the end of an era in railway history and would result in changes
in the duties of Henry Booth. On the 4th April 1846 the
Liverpool Mercury reported:

'On Tuesday a large number of the Directors and
principal Shareholders met in the Clarendon Rooms, South
John Street, for the purpose of considering the propriety of
presenting a testimonial of respect to Mr. Henry Booth, the
Secretary, and formerly Manager and Treasurer of the
Liverpool and Manchester Railway before its amalgam-
ation. The Chair was taken by Mr. Charles Lawrence,
(Chairman of the Grand Junction Board of Directors) by
whom the meeting was called. The Chairman, in a suitable
address, moved that a testimonial be presented to Mr.
Booth, and that a Committee of the Directors of the Grand
Junction, and those gentlemen who were on the late
Manchester and Liverpool Direction, be appointed a
Committee to carry out this object. Mr. John Moss,
Chairman of the late Direction for the Liverpool and
Manchester, seconded the resolution, which, after com-
mendatory speeches from other gentlemen, was carried
unanimously.'

*The Shareholders of the North Union Railway refused to agree to this
amalgamation, and as a result part of the line became joint with the London &
North Western and Lancashire & Yorkshire Railways.

Herapath's Journal and *Railway Magazine* of the 10th October 1846 contained the following note:

'We see with pleasure that a subscription has been commenced for Mr. Booth who for nearly twenty years has been connected with the Liverpool and Manchester Company. If any gentleman deserves a testimonial it is Mr. Booth, as he may from his long connection with these undertakings, be almost denominated the father of railway management.'

Mr. Hardman Earle was appointed Honorary Treasurer and at a meeting of the Committee at the end of September 1846 he reported that the subscriptions amounted to 3,000 guineas. Of this, 200 guineas were spent on an inscribed candelabrum, and a banker's order for the balance was sent to Henry Booth on the 12th October 1846.* The subscriptions ranged from 200 guineas from the Duke of Sutherland to five shillings each from a widow and two spinsters of Galway. There were subscriptions from his three brothers; £50 from Thomas, James sent £10; he had moved to London twenty-five years before, and Charles gave £25.

---

*The accompanying letter from Charles Lawrence, Henry Booth's reply and a copy of the inscription on the candelabrum are in Appendix VI.

Chapter IX

LONDON AND NORTH WESTERN RAILWAY

Although the Amalgamation Bill did not receive the Royal Assent until July 1846, the London & North Western Railway Board, consisting of eight Directors from the London & Birmingham and six from the Grand Junction Railways, met for the first time on the 13th December 1845. It was arranged that future meetings should be at Euston Station at 10 a.m. on the Saturday following the second Friday in each month, and on the previous days the committees were to meet to prepare for the Board Meeting. Under the Amalgamation Act, the Boards of the two railways carried on as local Boards, with their own committees, and only after five years were the local ones abolished and the main Board increased to thirty members.

At the first meeting, the principal officers, Mr. R. Creed of the London & Birmingham Railway and Captain Huish and Henry Booth of the Grand Junction Railway, were instructed to carry on their respective departments as they were then doing. In due course, Captain Huish was appointed General Manager and Mr. Creed and Henry Booth Joint Secretaries with their offices at Euston and Liverpool. There had been two schemes for the London & Birmingham Railway. Mr. Creed was the Secretary for one of them and became Secretary for the L&BR when the two projects joined forces. Mr. Creed had been a partner in a banking firm, but as he had been dissatisfied with the partnership, this had been dissolved. A few years later one of the partners was found guilty of

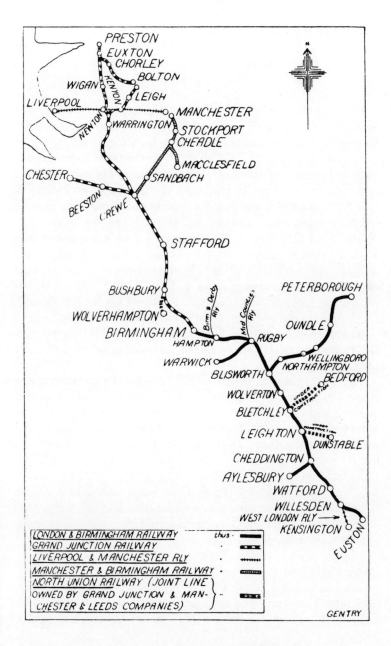

The railways that became the L&NWR system

malpractices during the period Mr. Creed had been a partner, and it was believed that as a result Mr. Creed lost £40,000. He retired in 1848 and died on the 22nd January 1867 at the age of 88; his wife, who was the same age, died seven hours afterwards.

Captain Mark Huish was born in Nottingham in 1808, and joined the East India Company's Bengal Army at the age of 16. He reached Calcutta at the end of the Burmese War. He learnt three native languages and attained the rank of Captain, but with no prospect of active service he returned home in 1835. In 1837 he was appointed Secretary of the Glasgow, Paisley & Greenock Railway, the Act for which had just been passed. When he left that railway to become the Secretary and Manager of the GJR in 1841, the proprietors presented him with a piece of plate. Captain Huish always preserved his military manner and bearing. He accomplished a vast amount of work and was something of a dictator. He was presented with a piece of plate by his brother officers on his retirement. He died four days before Mr. Creed in January 1867.*

At the meeting on the 10th January 1846 Mr. Creed and Henry Booth gave details of the financial engagements of their companies.

There was then a discussion concerning the inconvenience caused by almost every place having its own local time, and it was agreed to adopt London time at Liverpool and Manchester. As usual, Henry Booth held strong views on the subject and in June 1844 he had drafted a Petition to Parliament:

'. . . in favour of London Time being authorised by the Legislature to be used throughout the United Kingdom, instead of each Town having its own Time, and all varying with their respective longitudes.'

The L&MR Board ordered the Petition to be engrossed and sealed, and Lord Sandon and Sir Howard Douglas, the Liverpool MPs were requested to present it to Parliament and to the Post Master General. In 1847 Henry Booth published a

Railway News Vol. VIII pp. 72-3.

pamphlet: 'Uniformity of Time, considered especially in reference to Railway Transit and the operations of the Electric Telegraph'.* In the same year these efforts reached a satisfactory conclusion; the Directors' Report, read by Henry Booth to the L&NWR Annual Meeting on the 14th February 1848, detailed what had been achieved:

'The opening of the Trent Valley Railway** on the 1st December 1847 and the new Post Office arrangements required for the conveyance of the Mails by that Line, afforded a favourable opportunity for introducing uniformity of time between Railway and Post Office time; and for expressing of all local time, so far as practicable, in conformity with the longitude of Greenwich.*** In this arrangement the principal Railway Companies have concurred and the public authorities on the most important towns in connection with the great Lines of Railway (Liverpool, Manchester, Birmingham, Leeds etc. etc.) taking into consideration the public convenience of one common standard, by which to regulate the appointments of a commercial and locomotive people, cheerfully acquiesced in the views of the Railway Companies, thereby assisting them most materially to accomplish the desired alteration, without either public or private inconvenience.'

One effect of the prospective amalgamation had been that the express from London to Liverpool and Manchester had been accelerated in March 1846 by reducing delays at Birmingham; the time of the journey becoming 5¾ instead of 6 hours. Owing to bad weather before the opening of the Trent Valley line, the track was not fully consolidated, and in spite of the reduced distance, trains had to run at slower speeds, so that the time reverted to 6 hours and only in March 1848 was the journey again made in 5¾ hours. In June when the Board accepted a recommendation from Captain Huish that the running speed of express trains should be 41 m.p.h. the time

---

*A copy of this pamphlet has not been traced.
**From Rugby to Stafford direct.
***Only in 1880 was this arrangement legalized by Act of Parliament.

became 5½ hours.

Of the various committees, Henry Booth attended only those of the main Board and of the Northern Division, which comprised the Grand Junction and Manchester & Birmingham Railways.* He was obviously most interested in the Northern Locomotive Committee and the Crewe Committee. The Directors who were members of the latter committee were members of the Grand Junction local Board, and they were Charles Lawrence, his son G.H. Lawrence, Hardman Earle and Henry Booth's younger brother Thomas Booth.

On the death of their father, Thomas Booth had become senior partner in Thomas Booth & Company. In 1835 he was elected an Alderman by the Borough Council. He had always taken an active part in the Reform movement, so that when, after the passage of the Municipal Reform Bill, the first elections were held at the end of that year, and the Reformers captured 43 out of the 48 seats,** he was one of sixteen Aldermen elected by the new Council. He became a Council representative on the Dock Committee. His term of office as Alderman was to November 1841, but by that time the Conservatives had become the majority party and he was not re-elected.

The Directors of the Grand Junction Railway were not eligible for re-election after a certain period of time and a vacancy occurring in consequence of this rule, Thomas Booth was elected a member of that Board in August 1841 and became a member of the local Board on the formation of the London & North Western Railway. In 1851 he was elected to the L&NWR Board in place of a Liverpool Director, Mr. L. Mozley, who had died. Thomas Booth was a member of the General Locomotive Committee at Euston and attended both Board and Committee Meetings regularly until his death in February 1855.

The Crewe Committee met on Saturday mornings (usually at Crewe but occasionally at Liverpool). At the start Captain Huish, who had moved to London, attended the meetings

---

*The latter railway only ran from Manchester to Crewe.
**Charles Lawrence, Alderman and a former Mayor, lost his seat on this occasion, but was re-elected a Councillor the following year.

from time to time, but later he ceased to attend them. It was reputed that he and Henry Booth were never on good terms after the formation of the L&NWR and Captain Huish rarely attended the Northern Committee Meetings for which Henry Booth was responsible. The Committee received frequent letters from him, however, particularly when Northern Division trains were late arriving at Rugby, where the Southern Division started. The Crewe Committee spent much time demonstrating that the lateness was exaggerated and that their locomotives were not at fault. The line had only been opened for ten days when, on the 10th December 1847, the General Locomotive Committee complained of: '. . . the lamentable time keeping of express trains since the opening of the Trent Valley line . . .' Figures of locomotive failures on trains were given to the committee and these showed that the Northern Division, which had more locomotives, almost invariably had less locomotive failures than the Southern Division. On the instructions of the committee, Henry Booth drafted a form of guard's journal, in which the exact cause of delays could be recorded.

As the following extracts from a contemporary account* show, the Crewe Committee, in addition to supervising the workshops, which had been started by the GJR in 1843, was responsible for the town:

> 'The Company's workshops at Crewe consist of a Locomotive and of a Coach department. In the manufactories of the former are constructed as well as repaired the whole of the engines and tenders required for the Northern Division . . .'

> 'The number of workmen employed in the above department is 1600, their wages averaging 3800£. a fortnight. The accounts of these expenses, as also a book of "casualties", in which every accident to, as well as every delay of, a train is reported, are examined once a fortnight by a special committee of directors.'

Stokers and Pokers.

'About a hundred yards [from the workshops] there stands a plain neat building, erected by the Company, containing baths, hot, cold, and shower, for the workmen, as well as for their wives and daughters . . .'

'To a medical man the Company gives a house and a surgery, in addition to which he receives from every unmarried workman 1d. per week; if married, and with a family, 2d. per week; for which he undertakes to give attendance and medicine to whatever men, women, children, or babies of the establishment may require them. A clergyman, with an adequate salary from the Company, superintends three large day-schools for about three hundred boys, girls, and infants. There is also a library and mechanic's institute, supported by a subscription of about 10s. a year, at which a number of very respectable artificers, whose education when young was neglected, attend at night to learn, ab initio, reading, writing, and arithmetic. There is likewise a vocal and instrumental class, attended by a number of workmen, with their wives and daughters.'

'The town of Crewe contains 514 houses, one church, three schools and one town-hall, all belonging to the Company . . .'

On the 6th March 1855 the last recorded meeting of the Crewe Committee took place; some of the matters dealt with were as follows: Driver George Leigh of Preston appeared before the committee for disobeying orders on the 24th February and was reprimanded. For failing to stop at Holywell with the night mail to Holyhead, Driver J. Clarke and fireman J. Phillip were dismissed; the committee concluded that the men were asleep. Driver J. Greenate brought his engine on to the main line at Edge Hill in the way of a passenger train on the 16th February. In view of his previous good character, he only received a reprimand. Driver J. Barras from Shrewsbury, driver D. Avery and fireman R. Fielding from Edge Hill, Liverpool, were dismissed for drunkenness. Instructions were given to the carriage department that for every First Class and every Second Class carriage scrapped, two composite carriages should be built. The committee acceded to the request of the Presbyterian congregation of Crewe to use the Town Hall on 'the expected day of public humiliation and fasting'.

* * *

In 1844, after the depression of the first years of the 1840s, trade had begun to improve and by 1846 the railway mania of that year was in full swing. Bills were being presented to Parliament for railways which could serve no useful purpose but to intensify competition and reduce the profitability of the existing ones. In 1847 there were crop failures, particularly the potato harvest in Ireland, and revolutions in Europe, and as a result conditions in this country deteriorated and there was difficulty in raising capital.

In February 1848 the L&NWR Report to the Shareholders stated:

'In meeting the Proprietors on the present occasion the Directors have to report to them the position of the Company, after perhaps the most disastrous period on record in our commercial history, a period of enterprise, speculation and excitement, having been followed by its natural consequence, a season of extreme stagnation and unprecedented difficulties.'

The report continued that railway traffic was not as bad as was to be expected, passenger receipts being equal to those of the corresponding period of the previous year, while goods and coal receipts showed an increase. With the exception of two short lines to collieries:

'. . . the Directors are happy to inform the Meeting, that they have no intention of applying to Parliament for any new lines in the present session.'

By July the Directors felt that some actual steps needed to be taken to reassure investors in their railway, that money subscribed to it was being properly used, and the Board resolved that — Minute 587:

'Mr. Booth be placed in communication with the Board and Committee of all lines in the expenditure of which this Company is interested.'

This was followed by a list of thirteen railways. The resolution continued that:

'He will make a monthly report and from time to time report the state of expenditure of all lines in course of construction in which this Company is interested.'

In the report to the shareholders on the 11th August 1848, the Directors commented on the unfavourable state of trade, aggravated by the revolutionary state of the Continent. A small increase in traffic receipts (£1,108) and a larger fall in working expenses (£12,068) had been offset by a big increase in interest charges. With the opening of the Trent Valley line, it was no longer permissible to charge to capital the interest on the expenditure incurred, so that the net receipts were £23,425 down at £491,272, and the dividend for the half year was reduced from 4% to 3½%. The report continued:

'No new responsibilities needing further outlay of capital were incurred in the last 12 months, but as there are still sources of expenditure on lines with which the Company is connected, a careful revision of every existing engagement of that nature and a constant superintendence of the proceedings in each particular case is considered indispensable. The Directors, impressed with this conviction, have appointed Mr. H. Booth, a Director of the Company, in conformity with the Act of Parliament for the supervision and control of the expenditure on the Leeds & Dewsbury and Huddersfield & Manchester Sections,* (in the place of Mr. John Cropper, resigned) and generally under the authority of the Board for the objects stated; a duty for which his abilities and experience peculiarly qualify him; and they are persuaded that the Company cannot fail to

---

*The two railways were incorporated in 1845 and by the L&NWR Act of 1847 that company was to acquire them when they opened for traffic.

benefit by the arrangement.'

This announcement led to a misunderstanding — that Henry Booth was appointed a Director of the L&NWR. The actual intention is clear from Minute No. 639 of the Board Meeting on the 9th September:

'Impressed with the importance of a constant supervision of expenditure of capital on lines with which the Company is connected . . . [the Board] had selected Mr. Henry Booth for this duty from their knowledge of his ability, and tried experience in all matters concerned with railways, Mr. Booth in executing the new functions and duties assigned to him as local director continues to exercise the same general supervision and authority as heretofore as the immediate Representative of the Board.'

In the fourth article on Henry Booth in the issue of the *Railway News* of the 29th May 1869, Robert Smiles, the Editor, wrote:

'In October 1848, he was appointed a director [of the L&NWR], with equal deliberative privileges and increased executive powers.'

This article formed part of the *Memoir*, and the statement was copied in the *Dictionary of National Biography* and by subsequent writers.

However, as stated in the report, Henry Booth was appointed a Director of the Leeds & Dewsbury and Huddersfield & Manchester Railways in place of John Cropper. He was not a Director of the L&NWR. The position was that under the 1847 L&NWR Act that Company had to appoint Directors to the Leeds & Dewsbury and Huddersfield & Manchester Railways. A deputation from the Huddersfield line went to Liverpool in October 1847 and was told that the appointments would be made at the next L&NWR Board Meeting. However, the matter was passed over to the Grand Junction and Manchester & Birmingham local Boards for attention, and it was not until April 1848 that the appointments were confirmed — Minute No. 513:

> 'John Cropper and T. Thomasson to the Leeds &
> Dewsbury. John Cropper, T. Thomasson and Mr. Rawson
> to the Huddersfield & Manchester . . . in conformity with
> the provisions of the act of amalgamation to superintend the
> completion of the two lines.'

Next month, however, in Minute No. 533, it was reported that
Mr. John Cropper was unable to act as Director, and the local
Boards were asked to find a replacement. From 1846 to 1851
Mr. Cropper was a Director on the Grand Junction local
Board, and became a Director of the L&NWR when the
Board of that Company was enlarged in 1851.

It is clear from Henry Booth's Reports that constant
supervision of capital expenditure should have started far
earlier; although he was able to save considerable sums, much
more could have been achieved if he had been called in before
the work being done had reached an advanced stage. One
instance was the excessive prices paid for land in the
Birmingham area, where the Great Western Railway was
expanding and buying up land. The L&NWR interests
required land there for which the estimated cost was £316,000,
but the price actually paid was £800,000. A further example
was at Huddersfield, where a far too elaborate station had
been constructed; it was twice as large as was likely to be
needed. To avoid pulling half the building down, it was agreed
that it should be completed and the centre part used as an
hotel and the surplus waiting rooms and booking office space
for the goods department.

Henry Booth's first report was dated the 4th September 1848
after he had made visits to the Huddersfield & Manchester
Railway and to the Manchester, South Junction & Altrincham
Railway; on one occasion attending a meeting of the Board of
the latter railway. On the first line, as the work done had been
over-valued, the full amount of the contract price — £270,000
— had already been paid to the contractor, and work
estimated at a further £50,000 to £60,000 was needed to
complete the line. The matter was being submitted to a
Referee for settlement. On the Altrincham line a badly

designed bridge in Manchester which could have been strengthened, had been scrapped at a cost of £1,200, and working out an improved design had caused further delay. At Altrincham an elaborate station had been started, the cost being disproportionate to the needs of the traffic. It was arranged to suspend the work while a plan was prepared for a light timber building, avoiding the massive arches and pillars in the original design.

Henry Booth also visited the Rugby & Stamford line, which was two thirds completed. He commented that the line ran through thinly populated agricultural land, which would produce only a small traffic, so that every economy was needed in the construction of the stations, and in running the line.

His remarks about the Rugby & Leamington line were scathing. The estimate for this line was £460,000, and £260,000 had already been spent.

'The question for consideration regarding this Line, are of a graver and more complex character. The country is a succession of undulations, and the operations, in consequence, unavoidably heavy; indeed the problem to discover justification for so extravagent an undertaking can find its solution only in the universal infatuation which prevailed in 1845 and 1846 — Extensive Viaducts, heavy embankments, Cuttings 60 feet deep, works scarcely warranted by a Traffic, such as exists between London & Birmingham or Liverpool & Manchester are now being constructed on a second or third competing Line to Leamington. The works have been delayed partly from financial considerations and partly in the expectation that the Great Western Railway would purchase or lease the Line.

'Meanwhile the Expenditure month by month is going on, not rapidly, but constantly without any definite or acknowledged object in view — Had there been a reasonable prospect of the Line, when completed yielding the most moderate return, the course would have been comparatively clear — but Captain Huish in his report read to the Board in February last, expressed his opinion that if completed, the Line could not be worked to any pecuniary profit — that a heavy loss is unavoidable but that further outlay will but increase that loss.

'I have therefore felt it my duty to suggest the expediency of the Board deciding upon the alternatives which may be considered as still open to them — whether to proceed with the works subject to such further outlay as may be required, or to cease operations, and save the remaining £200,000; — pausing till some arrangement can be made with the Great Western Company, or till there be a prospect of obtaining some return, if not on the whole outlay on the Line, at least for the money still to be expended.'

Henry Booth's October report covered a further visit to Manchester, South Junction & Altrincham Railway, where he had attended a committee meeting at which savings of £3,000 at the Oxford Road Station in Manchester had been agreed and the sum of £8,000 was to be realized by the sale of surplus land. When in London for the L&NWR Board Meeting in September, he had inspected the East and West India Dock Railway, and he was happy to say that the engineers in charge of this line were assiduous in keeping expenditure down. The work was being carried out in a simple and substantial manner free from unnecessary ornament and expense.

He had attended two Board Meetings of the Manchester & Huddersfield Railway when it had been reported that the tunnel at Huddersfield was fourteen to fifteen feet out of line laterally, and it was estimated that it would cost £1,500 to put it right. The Resident Engineer had been given notice of dismissal.

After a visit to the Birmingham Extension and Stour Valley Line from Birmingham to Wolverhampton where the land was costing far more than had been estimated he wrote:

'I propose to institute a strict analysis of the several contracts with a view to ascertain where the excess lies. . . . The population through this district is dense, compared with that in an Agricultural Country — but it is altogether of a low description, and what its locomotive tendencies may be remains to be seen.'

With the Secretary and the Engineer he had ridden over a portion of the Buckingham lines from Bletchley to Banbury; work on the branch to Oxford had been suspended. He reported:

'Banbury is an Agricultural Market Town, of about 8,000 inhabitants — where large cattle fairs* are held monthly — This place is to the Buckingham Lines, what Market Harborough is to the Rugby and Stamford. Both are Agricultural and Grazing districts, to which a Railway will be a great accommodation; but in regard to which, it is still a question how far the Traffic will yield a remunerative return. Total estimated cost £1,445,438 of which £600,000 has been spent. . . . a moderate return might be anticipated from a strictly economical completion of the Line and subsequent working of the Traffic; the *Oxford and Rugby Line* from Banbury to Oxford constitutes at once, a duplicate and rival communication with London. Possibly before either Railway is opened the Relations between this Company and the Great Western may be such as to prevent the exhibition of two great Companies waging a hostile competition for the Banbury Traffic.'

In November, with Mr. Thomasson and the Resident Engineer, he inspected the Manchester, South Junction & Altrincham Railway and commented that the bulk of the passenger traffic would be to Bowden just beyond Altrincham:

'The Character of Bowden as a residence is peculiar — situate in the midst of a low flat country for many miles round. The Parish Church occupies the crown of a Knoll of high ground with beautiful slopes on all sides, affording admirable sites for Building and already occupied to a considerable extent in this way — It is a Sandy healthy Soil and the spot was of old described as the Bowden Downs. It is on the highway from Manchester to Knutsford and is contiguous to Dunham Park the seat of Lord Stamford.

*This fair, now a weekly market, exists to this day and is reputed to be the largest in Europe.

Here the Merchants and Manufacturers of Manchester resort to escape from the smoke of the Town and the fogs of the low country in the intermediate District; and here the artisans and working population repair in great numbers for health and recreation on Sundays and Holydays — As this takes place at present with the imperfect means of communication afforded by Canal and Omnibuses there can be no doubt that this kind of intercommunication will largely increase after the opening of the Railway.'

Of the Birmingham Extension and Stour Valley Railway he wrote:

'On the 14th November I attended the Jury case or Inquisition at Birmingham, into the value of the property required by the Company from the Trustees of the Free Grammar School for the proposed new Railway Station in that Town — The result of the Inquiry throws some light on the extraordinary Expenditure for *Land* on the Stour Valley Line, into which I have previously instituted an investigation.

'The Verdict of the Jury . . . is one of the most remarkable that has occurred amongst the numerous instances of extortion from Railway Companies. — The property in question consists partly of vacant Land but principally of Houses of the lowest description, many of them being occupied as Brothels or Beer Shops. — It appeared that the Trustees of the Free Grammar School had been most anxious to purge the immediate neighbourhood of the School from so foul a contamination, but this they had been able to effect, only in a very limited degree: the distant *Reversion* only of these Premises belonging to the Trustees, while the present occupancy was altogether independent of their control — Under these circumstances great was the satisfaction of the Free Grammar School Trustees when the Railway Company proposed to come in that direction and sweep from the ground the notorious and long standing nuisance, so sensible of this was the late Head Master, Dr. Lee, the present Bishop of Manchester that he gave evidence in Parliament in favour of a measure so beneficial to the School. Notwithstanding these facts, the Trustees claimed, and the Jury awarded, not only an extravagantly high value for the property; but 50 per Cent in addition, under the unwarrantable pretence of compensation for *compulsory Sale* — £26,000 being awarded as the market value of the Premises, and £13,000, in addition, for compulsory Sale.

'The first question to be solved after so iniquitous a verdict, was the possibility of obtaining a new Trial — But after a full consideration, the Lawyers decided there was no ground in Law for setting aside the present Verdict.

'This anomaly in our Jurisprudence, calls for the serious consideration of Railway Companies as well as of the Railway Commissioners . . . .

'. . . in an Inquiry into the value of Property required under an Act of Parliament for some public purpose, where Tens of thousands may be involved in the issue, and where the Court of Inquiry is not presided over by a Judge of the Land, but by a person styled an assessor, who may or may not be competent for the Office, however glaring the misdirection of the assessor or however monstrous the Verdict of the Jury, the decision is final . . . .

'This is a Line from Wolverhampton to Birmingham about 14 miles in length — the unfortunate peculiarity of it being it is a duplicate Line with the Birmingham and Oxford, and Oxford Worcester and Wolverhampton Lines through the same district — the latter Line being in fact a triplicate route almost from Wolverhampton to Dudley . . .

'But the most extensive link in this group of Lines is that portion of the Birmingham and Oxford Line through the town of Birmingham and the immediate vicinity; a distance of about 3 miles the cost of which including the Station in Birmingham cannot be estimated under £500,000 — The corresponding or duplicate portion, of the Stour Valley and Birmingham Extension Lines is in a state of great forwardness, and any important saving of Capital to the LNWCo must be by a union of the Birmingham and Oxford with the Stour Valley Line . . . In making one Line and one Station suffice for that District, and by each Co. participating in the saving to be so effected. For this purpose an arrangement with the GWCo would of course be necessary.'

He reported further on the 7th February 1849:

'The first subject to which I would at this time request the attention of the Board is the late Jury case at Birmingham; an enquiry into the value of certain Lands and Premises required by the Company from Capt. Inge —
'. . . the palpable injustice complained of, in the case of the Free Grammar School, consisted in adopting the rule laid down by a Committee of the House of Lords, of first awarding a high value for the land taken and then adding 50 per cent for what is termed compulsory Sale.

'A moment's reflection will show that this rule, proclaimed ex Cathedra by a Committee of the Lords is altogether devoid of reason or principle, even when applied to Landed Estates to which it was intended to have a more immediate reference . . . in the case of the Free Grammar School property . . . where whole streets of worn out and dilapidated Buildings were to be purchased, and of which the full value was £20,000, to add to this sum, 50 per cent . . . constituted an absurd and flagrant injustice . . .

'Warned by the result of the former inquiry, that it was in vain to trust to the evidence of the local Surveyors . . . it was considered essential to obtain evidence from a distance.

'Mr. Stewart from Liverpool and Mr. Tite and Mr. Bedd from London accordingly assisted at the Investigation which took place on Tuesday and Wednesday, the 30th and 31st January — Mr. Talbot, the Barrister, being the assessor — the claimants witnesses declared the value of the property including compulsory sale to be £22,500 — The real value being about £12,000 — Mr. Stewart and Mr. Tite gave evidence, as to the correct principle on which the valuation should be founded, and against the unwarranted addition for compulsory sale.

'The Assessor complimented both these Witnesses on the clear evidence which they had given; and himself ridiculed the rule attempted to be established by a Committee of the Lords. But the Company had already been committed too far by their own Surveyors. . . . and the Jury gave their Verdict for £16,800.'

In June he reported that engines and carriages were proceeding along the whole length of the Huddersfield & Manchester line and it was hoped to open it on the 2nd July:

'In the Standedge Tunnel which is three miles long and consists of a single Line of way the Electric Telegraph has been put up, and messages conveyed with great accuracy between Stations at each End — the wires are protected from moisture and the insulation effectually secured, by the new covering Gutta percha, which promises to answer the desired object very satisfactorily — some degree of uncertainty however must be admitted to attend the operation of the Electric Telegraph in Tunnels — At the present time the Electric Telegraph Company are constructing their sixth set of wires through the Kilsby Tunnel [near Northampton], five sets having failed — and at present so little confidence has the operating Engineer in their sixth Experiment that he is employing 16 wires apparently in the hope that some, out of so large a number will succeed.'

In this connection, in February 1851, three Directors and Henry Booth were appointed to consider and enter into arrangements with the Electric Telegraph Company. Progress was so rapid that in January 1855 when Captain Huish inaugurated a monthly meeting of Managers at Birmingham, he called the attention of the various officers entitled to use the telegraph, that it should not be used for unimportant messages, which could, if forwarded in ample time, go by train, and he stressed the need for condensation of words in telegrams.

During 1849 Henry Booth wrote thirty-one letters to Mr. W. Eagle Bott, the Secretary of the Leeds & Dewsbury Railway, and these letters, in his own handwriting, are in the Public Record Office.* It must be assumed that similar letters to

*PRO file — Rail 410/1578.

those written to Mr. Bott were sent to the Secretaries of the other railways with which he was dealing. In the case of the Leeds & Dewsbury, the line was nearing completion, and many of the letters were requests for figures of costs and explanations regarding them. Several of the letters are of more general interest and the first of these, dated the 19th January 1849, reads:

> 'It has been mentioned to me that the Dewsbury Line is in a very rough state & in some places, hardly safe — I presume the contractors have the charge of it, and I am afraid they will spend as little money as possible, on the maintenance of the way — It is a very important matter, however, and I shall be obliged to you to insist upon the several contractors doing their duty — In a wet season like this, a great deal of upholding is absolutely essential.'

On the 22nd January 1849 he wrote that on the following Thursday he was going to Leeds for a meeting of the Joint Station Committee, on which he was the L&NWR representative. He had arranged with Mr. Hawkshaw to provide an engine and carriage to meet the 10.15 a.m. train from Manchester at Mirfield, and wanted Mr. Bott to join them at Mirfield for the trip to Leeds.* On the 26th he wrote a letter regarding his return journey:

> 'In passing over the Dewsbury Line, yesterday, it seemed to me that in the Rock Cutting, not very far from Batley, the Contractor has left the rock in a dangerous state, as regards our trains. It is in large irregular & broken stratifications, many large masses, 20 ft. above the rails, being apparently ready to fall, after a very little frost, or other cause —
> 'I shall be obliged to you to have this looked to, and if there be cause for apprehension to have it removed.'

---

*Originally the L&YR reached Leeds via Normanton and the North Midland Railway. When the L&DR was opened, it was leased by the L&YR, as the distance from Mirfield to Leeds — 12½ miles — was half that of the previous route. Mr. Hawkshaw was the L&YR's Engineer.

A new subject appeared on the 7th February:

'I return you the plans & designs of Cottages, per Parcel, this Evening.

'You seem to me to have crimped these dwellings, rather too much, and that they ought to be a little more spacious, or rather a little less contracted — if you see your way to a clear Rent of 6%, instead of 8 or 9, I think that is what should be aimed at — I would not build *at all, for the sake* of Rent; but only where the men suffered serious inconvenience for want of decent habitations.

'After considering the matter perhaps you will tell me how many Cottages, & where, & for what cost, your Committee recommend, to be built.'

On the 2nd April, there was more about the cottages:

'The plans of the Cottages I think will do with one or two slight alterations, which I have explained to Mr. Child.

'One point I omitted to ascertain, indeed there was no section to show it — I mean the *height* of the rooms — I am a great friend to light ventilation etc & I have begged Mr. Child to put larger windows in some of the Bed rooms & connected with this is the height of the rooms — which in cottages is very much stunted. Bed rooms should be 8 foot high & lower story 9.

'I told Mr. Child we should only have 4 Cottages instead of 6 at Batley — Of course we must only build for our own people.'

A letter on the 12th February dealt with the usual problem of estimates being exceeded:

'I beg to acknowledge rect. of your favour . . . inclosing Statement of account, showing amount of expenditure to the 31/1/49 and estimated cost of completing the line — £1,044,000 is an awful amount, on an Estimate of *£600,000* I trust every effort has been made & will be to cut down the exorbitant and unjust demands of Contractors. If £90,000 be due to Contractors, they ought to be very wealthy to remain out of their money without inconvenience; I confess I am very suspicious on this front: which makes a contract for a specific sum, much more satisfactory to me than one depending on disputed measurements.'

In April, Mr. Bott mismanaged a rate demand; without mentioning the matter to Henry Booth, this was passed on to the Lancashire & Yorkshire Railway, which was leasing the line, and several L&YR Directors complained to him about the matter at a meeting. Henry Booth wrote to Mr. Bott on the 23rd April and explained that a large deduction from any rating assessment was allowable for expenses, and if the time for doing so had not expired, it was desirable to appeal against the assessment. The letter ended on another subject:

'As to the Morley Goods Shed, I should be glad to see a plan of what you propose to do, or to recommend. Is there any great interchange of traffic between Morley & Leeds. And supposing we allow Thompson the Contractor to excavate the ground for the sake of the Stone — how is the Stone to be conveyed to Leeds?

'I will require an accurate plan & section of the ground to be excavated, if Mr. Thompson is to do it.

'But the first thing to be satisfied about, is, will there be traffic sufficient to justify the outlay?'

In 1850 the L&NWR dispensed with the services of Mr. Bott, and he was given compensation for the loss of his position.

After the completion of the various railways on which he reported to the Board, Henry Booth was called upon to prepare reports on a number of problems as they arose. On a superannuation scheme in 1852 — the Birkenhead Docks in 1853 — on the profitability of steamboats worked jointly with the L&YR between Fleetwood and Belfast in 1855 — but the most important matter which he investigated was on the re-laying of the permanent way in November 1855.

As was the case with the L&MR, in order to save expense many of the railways built in the period before 1846 had been laid with lighter rails than were desirable. In consequence of this, after its formation in 1846, the L&NWR had to re-lay the bulk of its lines. Each year provision had been made for the cost of this work, and the problem was whether the amount charged to running expenses was adequate; some of the work done represented improvements which could be charged to capital.

The result of Henry Booth's calculations was that in future £110,000 should be put aside each year as renewals and £25,000 charged to capital, on the assumption that the life of the new track would be fifteen years. This conclusion meant that in the eight years to 1855 too much had been charged to capital and, in consequence, an extra amount needed to be charged to revenue in the next seven years.

* * *

The Caledonian Railway from Carlisle to Glasgow and Edinburgh was opened in 1848. The L&NWR was keenly interested in opening up traffic to Scotland, and subscribed for a considerable number of shares in the company. By 1850 the Caledonian was in financial difficulties, and in February a new Board was elected. The old Board had given guarantees, and entered into commitments to preferential creditors, which could not possibly be met, as receipts did not cover expenses. A reconstruction of the company and fresh capital was needed, if it was to continue in business; this the new Board endeavoured to arrange with the various classes of creditor.

In the L&NWR Report, read by Henry Booth at the half-yearly meeting on the 16th August, reference was made to negotiations with the Caledonian leased and guaranteed lines, where concessions were needed, if the L&NWR was to get some return on the capital invested. At the L&NWR Board Meeting on the 14th September, the matter was brought up by Mr. William Rotheram; it was decided that it was essential that there should be a strong and united Board to manage the Caledonian Railway, and that every effort should be made to bring about an amicable adjustment to the various and complicated questions involved in the disputes.

On the 27th September the half-yearly meeting of

M

Caledonian shareholders took place, and there were more changes in the membership of the Board. A poll was demanded on whether the report should be accepted. The result was that a majority of shareholders was in favour — majority 2185 — but when calculated on the value of shares held, £785,090 were against and £773,802 in favour.

At the L&NWR Board Meeting on the 12th October, it was reported that the Caledonian had refused the offer of assistance and that the Chairman had resigned. On the 9th November there was a further discussion and the Board resolved that — Minutes 1369 - 1371:

'Captain Carnegie, Mr. William Rotheram and Mr. Henry Booth be requested to accept temporarily if offered seats in the Direction of the Caledonian Railway — the former as Chairman, if that be the desire of his colleagues in general — with a view to assisting in the amicable completion without further delay of satisfactory arrangements in that undertaking and rescuing it from its present lamentable and anomalous position.'

The Board would support the three in any arrangement made, and there would be a transfer of sufficient of the L&NWR Caledonian Stock to qualify them as Directors, and, finally, they would be indemnified by the L&NWR in respect of their acts.

On the 14th December Captain Carnegie reported the failure of the mission to obtain any agreement. He and his colleagues were requested to retain their seats until the end of the year, and then to resign if they saw no hope of success in the objects for which they were appointed.

In the Caledonian Report to the Shareholders Meeting on the 28th March 1851 it was stated that:

'In December, 1850, three Directors from the London and North Western Company joined the Caledonian Board, and as members thereof, and in co-operation with other Caledonian Directors, offered a scheme of general arrangement to the guaranteed and preference Shareholders, but which the latter unanimously refused. The three London and North Western Directors having failed in their object withdrew from the Board. . . . The Directors acknowledge the valuable services of the members of the London and North Western Board of Directors in December last, as well as since that time, in efforts made to conclude amicable arrangements with the guaranteed and preference Shareholders.'

Eventually, in May 1851, a compromise was reached between all parties to the dispute; a Bill to enable the Caledonian Railway to raise loans of £650,000 was agreed, and as a result the restructuring of the company's indebtedness became possible.

* * *

In September 1850 the L&NWR Board received notice from a Mr. Richard Moon* of his intention to be a candidate for a directorship. The following year he became a Director and was elected Chairman in 1861. It has been noted in the index on the file of his letters preserved in the Public Record Office** that:

'Those written to the Marquis of Chandos (Chairman 1854-61) are notable for their vigour and candour in his zeal for reorganisation and economy.'

The following extract from a letter written to the Chairman on the 5th May 1857 is evidence of the need for reorganization:

'. . . the flourishing state of the country . . . our beggarly 5% dividend.'

Mr. Moon made every effort to reduce expenditure, although it might sometimes have been of advantage to the company to adopt a more generous attitude. He could not proceed with the economies he desired until he became

---

*Richard Moon was born in 1814, retired from the L&NWR in 1891 and died in 1899. He was created a Baronet in 1887, Golden Jubilee year.
**PRO file — Rail 1008/101.

Chairman, but his influence was evident before then, as shown in the following instance in February 1858 when Henry Booth sent a recommendation to the Board:

> 'That free passes for a limited distance be allowed under regulations to enable Station Masters and others in rural districts to send their Boys to School.'

The recommendation was turned down, although it would have cost nothing, and would have removed one of the disadvantages to staff sent to out-of-the-way places.

There was also the case of a fire at Conway Station in December 1858, in which the Station Master lost property to the value of £107.8.0d. It was proposed to the Board that he should receive £75 compensation, but an amendment was moved for the sum to be £50, and this was lost by only eight votes to eleven.

Writing to the Chairman on the 6th September 1858 Mr. Moon describes how the Duke of Wellington had conducted his campaign against the French in the Peninsular War in 1812 and 1813:

> '. . . checked everything himself, . . . got rid of every fellow that was idle, wicked or thoughtless & by the time they had got to the battle of Salamanca he went to bed & going said to the Aide de Camp tell Lord — I shall move the army in the morning — everything was prepared, & he had no occasion to do it himself & the army did move.
>
> 'This is what we must do . . . have good tools to work with giving every soul in the establishment to understand the interest of the Company must not be trifled with . . . I sincerely trust that you will have courage to go through with it. . . .'

These plans for radical changes were bound to produce opposition from the older members of the staff, who could not be expected to see eye to eye with the military discipline envisaged by Richard Moon. He makes spiteful remarks in the letter about the two senior managers, Captain Huish and Henry Booth. Captain Huish was about to retire, and the letter gives advice to Lord Chandos on the remarks he should make at the Board Meeting:

'You must not be content with Huish, don't say much about his good qualities for as to management he has known none.'

He continues:

'Booth who is worse than useless & positively obstructive must go —'

A remark a little later in the letter may have a bearing on the use of the word 'obstructive':

'. . . no-one shall be in a position quietly and unseen to thwart your measures.'

In his letter Mr. Moon also makes clear his opinion of various other members of the staff:

'Mills, Horne, Cooper, Bruyere by degrees we must weed them all.'

The Booth characteristic of obstinacy would certainly have been a serious obstacle to a new style of management; however, Henry Booth would be retiring shortly. Mr. Creed had retired when he was 70. Henry Booth would be 70 in April 1859 and in January of that year he wrote to Lord Chandos in this connection. His letter was reported to the Board on the 9th April and it was resolved — Minute 3543:

'That Mr. Booth's request to be allowed to retire and to receive the sum of £5,000 in consideration of his past services, and in lieu of any retiring Salary be accepted, and that the Board feel it to be but an act of justice to avail themselves of this opportunity to Express their sense of the Eminent zeal, ability, and industry displayed by Mr. Booth during the long and faithful Services which he has rendered to the Liverpool and Manchester, and subsequently to the

London and North Western Railway Company, during a period of thirty three years.'*

On the 6th June the Chairman mentioned that Mr. Booth had returned the passes lately held by him as Secretary, and it was resolved unanimously:

'That the passes of the London and North Western Railway be returned to Mr. Booth with a request that he will continue to hold them.'

Henry Booth attended the Northern Sub-Committee in Liverpool for the last time on the 25th May. He called the attention of the Committee to the fact that he was the Licensee of the Refreshment Room at Lime Street Station and it was arranged that the Licence should be transferred to Mr. Norris, one of his assistants. It was agreed at the meeting that £50 should be advanced to Mr. Samuel Wells, contractor for a well at Earlestown. The money was needed to pay wages the next day, and the amount due to Mr. Wells from Euston would not arrive in time.

The occasion for it is not known, but a presentation was made to Henry Booth in 1853 and Smiles wrote of this:

'In 1853 Mr. Booth received a gratifying mark of esteem and respect from his brother officers in the presentation of an elegant timepiece and a number of bronze statuettes.'**

---

*Smiles's *Memoir* stated that the Board presented Henry Booth prior to his retirement with 5,000 guineas and this was repeated by the DNB and other writers. The statement was shown to be incorrect when the Minutes of the Board of the L&NWR became available.

**Two of these statuettes are in the possession of the author and are the work of Antonin Moine (1797-1849) the French sculptor and painter. He produced a great number of 'statuettes très recherchées', and sculptures by him are in the Place de la Concorde and the Luxembourg Museum in Paris.

Chapter X

Henry Booth wrote four pamphlets between 1847 and 1854 and two of these were addressed to Lord Campbell to point out the inequity of his 'Death by Accidents Compensation Act'.

Of the other two, the first published in 1847, 'The Rationale of the Currency Question', was a polemic against the deflationary policy of the Bank of England, caused by the loss of gold reserves, which had resulted in the discount rate rising to 4% in 1846. With further increases in 1847, the discount rate for good bills had reached 8% in October. The Banking Act of 1844, which made Bank of England notes convertible into gold, had not provided the Bank with enough resources to be a bank of issue and carry out its ordinary banking business. The need was for a national bank, run by Parliamentary Commissioners, to hold foreign securities.

In the Introduction to 'Master and Man', published in 1853, he wrote:

'I have thought that some of the important questions, which agitate the minds of the working classes, might be discussed in the form of familiar dialogue.

'The labouring population of the present day are deeply interested in a variety of subjects requiring close thought for their right understanding, and which thirty years ago would have been considered of too abstruse a character to be canvassed, except by philosophers or statesmen. But in our commercial and manufacturing districts, the operatives have become readers and thinkers, and instances are not uncommon where great acuteness has been displayed by the workman or artisan, in the discussion of grave national questions, whether of social economy or of general politics. . . . It will appear from the conversations on what points Man differs from Man, and how by friendly discussion of the matters at issue, we may hope such differences will be narrowed, mutual confidence restored, and a right understanding be established between them.'

Topics discussed in the booklet were:
The Franchise and the Ballot
Competition, Supply and Demand, Capital and Labour
Population, Education, Emigration, and the Poor Laws.
Amongst other points made, the following problems are still with us. The hope was expressed that:

'. . . intimidation by landlords and employers, a moral wrong, which has grown lately, will diminish in view of the kindly feeling between employers and employed . . .
'. . . in a satisfactory state of our social system, in which the conditions of well being should be duly observed, and should result in the prosperity of the whole community, free and open voting . . . would be most congenial to the spirit of our Constitution; and, assisted by discussion and universal expression of sentiment on the leading topics of the day, open voting would tend to establish a sound and independent public opinion. To exchange this . . . for a system of secret voting would be a serious evil.'

His view on the secret ballot might well be considered by those who currently believe it to be a panacea for industrial troubles.
The following quotations are of interest, the second one repeating his views on no one marrying before he can afford it:

'In the early days of aerostation, a student of Natural Philosophy made his first ascent in a balloon. The balloon burst because of the expansion of the hydrogen, there being no method to release it, and the balloonist forfeited his life by violation of a natural law. . . .'

'. . . foolish for a man of twenty and a girl of nineteen to
marry . . . the man should work three to four years saving a
third of his wages . . . till he could see his way to enter the
joys and cares and duties and responsibilities of matrimony.'

John Campbell, later Lord Campbell, was a clever young
Scotsman, who came to London to tutor in 1798 when he was
18 years old. His parents intended him to become a minister,
but when he had been in London a little while, he persuaded
them to let him go to the Bar. From November 1800, while
studying at Lincoln's Inn, he maintained himself by reporting
the debates of the House of Commons and cases in the Law
Courts for the *Morning Chronicle*. Campbell did not know
shorthand, but felt that rewriting the speeches from notes gave
a better effect than the exact words. He specialized in
reporting commercial law cases, which, during the Napoleonic
Wars, became increasingly important. He was called to the
Bar in 1806 and in a few years built up a reputation in
mercantile law. In due course, Campbell became a Member of
Parliament; in 1833 he was made Solicitor General and in
1834 Attorney General. Campbell's real interest was in law
reform, and in 1835 he was responsible for persons charged
with felonies being given the right to address juries, through
counsel or in person, and to receive copies of depositions or
inspect them, which had not previously been allowed.

In 1841 Campbell was appointed Lord Chancellor of
Ireland. This position had always previously been held by an
Irishman and there was such an outcry that he only held the
office for six weeks. For many years he hoped to be made Lord
Chief Justice, but it was not until 1850 that he achieved this
ambition and, eventually, at the age of 80, he was made Lord
Chancellor, dying two years later.

In the period 1842 to 1846 Lord Campbell was responsible
for three important acts to improve the law. In 1842 a
Copyright Act, a Libel Act in 1843 and in 1846 the 'Death by
Accidents Compensation Act' and, finally, in 1857 an Obscene
Publications Act. The last three were all known as Lord
Campbell's Acts.

Before 1846 anyone who was injured in an accident could claim compensation from those responsible, but if he was killed no compensation could be obtained by his heirs or executors. The law was that when someone was killed by the fault of another, say in a railway accident, the coroner's jury was entitled to confiscate the instrument by which the death had been caused — a deodand. In the case of railways, if an engine was at fault, it could then be redeemed by payment of a sum fixed by the jury and the proceeds went either to the Lord of the Manor or the Crown.

On the 2nd August 1845 an accident occurred at Chalk Farm on the London & Birmingham Railway. The night mail and passenger train from Liverpool was running a quarter of an hour ahead of time and there was early morning fog. The first goods train (2 engines 47 wagons) of the day to Birmingham was due to leave at 4.15 a.m. but at 5.3 a.m. its last wagons having only just been picked up, it was crossing the up line when the mail train hit the third wagon from the engine. Mr. Charles Dean, a promising young barrister, was injured in the collision and died later in the day. At the inquest it appeared that no warning signs had been hoisted by the policeman (signalman) on duty at the crossing. In his evidence, the policeman, J. Halse, said that due to extra goods being taken, there was a delay in starting such trains. The jury decided that Mr. Dean died from injuries due to a collision near Campden Town and made a deodand on engine No. 91 of the London & Birmingham Railway for £1,000, which, in this case, went to the Crown and was, therefore, of no benefit to Mr. Dean's family. The jury felt that the London & Birmingham Railway's laws and regulations for the guidance of their servants had been carried out very inefficiently for some time past.

General Pasley, the inspecting officer, stated in his report that in clear weather the signal at the crossing was visible to drivers of up trains on emerging from Primrose Hill Tunnel 506 yards away, and that there should be no difficulty in stopping a train before the crossing. Although he was travelling quite slowly, the driver of the mail train was mainly to blame. As he had not passed the goods train, he should have realized that it might be blocking the crossing. Mr. Creed, who had visited the scene of the accident with General Pasley, took the view that the real cause was the failure of the policeman to exhibit a signal at the exit from the tunnel, in conformity with the original L&MR rule on the protection of trains stopping in foggy weather. General Pasley commented adversely on the delays in starting trains from London, which were due to a large increase in traffic following reductions in fares and rates.

Clearly Lord Campbell's action at the beginning of 1845 in bringing in the 'Deodand Abolition Bill' and the 'Death by Accidents Compensation Bill' to replace it was proved to be justified. However, Lord Campbell was not liked in the House of Commons, and the Bills were not proceeded with when they were sent down to them, so that they lapsed.

In 1846 Lord Campbell introduced the Bills into the House of Lords again and, in due course, they were passed and sent to the Commons on the 7th May. Over two months elapsed before the Commons dealt with the Bills, but they were passed, although there was much grumbling about the short time there was to consider the 'Death by Accidents Compensation Bill' before the end of the session. This Bill was sent back to the Lords on the 8th August and received the Royal Assent on the 16th August.

In 1845 the L&MR was interested both in its own Bill for various extensions and in the Bill to amalgamate with the Grand Junction Railway. The Grand Junction and the London & Birmingham Railway Amalgamation Bill was going through Parliament in 1846 and it was not until 1849 that the full implications of Lord Campbell's Act were realized.

In a report to the L&NWR Board in February 1849, dealing with the desirability of insurance companies offering policies to compensate railway travellers for death or injury in accidents, Henry Booth wrote:

'I conceive, however, that it is decidedly the interest of Railway Companies to encourage any well devised scheme for effecting the object proposed — At present the operation of what is termed Lord Campbell's Act, is a palpable injustice to Railway Companies. . . . But the principle on which Lord Campbell's Act is administered violates every principle of commercial justice.'

However, it was not until 1852 that he found opportunity to write his first pamphlet on this subject. This was in the form of a letter signed 'Shareholder' and began by pointing out the great changes in our measure of time and distance brought about by railways, and that without personal experience, few can realize what other people and places are like, or how much the bonds of amity between nation and nation and man to man and the diffusion of information had progressed. Further advantages had been the reduction of prices of commodities, the Penny Post, and the Great Exhibition of 1851 when vast numbers of people were enabled to visit it by the provision of cheap excursions to London.

Reference was then made to the fact that in the four years to 1850 the total fatal casualties on railways to passengers, staff and trespassers had averaged 217 annually; the number of passengers killed averaging 25. This was compared with fatalities on British ships at sea, which averaged 3,377 annually during the same period and an estimated number of all deaths by violence in the United Kingdom in 1850 of 20,000. Railway servants were selected to be sober, industrious and energetic and were paid good wages and had to obey strict rules of punctuality, sobriety and obedience, but men were sometimes frail and imperfect. Even with the utmost care to obtain the best material and workmanship, machines might suffer from unexplained and startling failures, and railway travellers were well aware that there was no absolute immunity from casualties.

At this point Henry Booth returns to the matter he stressed in his letter to the Irish Railway Commissioners, that where one line will be sufficient for the traffic, it is undesirable to build a second line. While with the first railways the legislature had wanted proof that there would be enough traffic to make a line profitable, by 1852 competition had become a major concern. He commented that:

'The expenditure of capital without adequate return is confessedly a waste of national resources which it is the duty of Parliament to prevent.'

He continues that in 1841, under Lord Seymour's Act, the Railway Accident Inspectorate was set up to ensure that, should an accident occur, steps would be taken to prevent similar ones in future, while Lord Campbell's Act laid responsibilities on the railways for fatal accidents, which were not previously attached to them, although the older railways had had certain responsibilities placed upon them. The alteration in the law was to be expected, but it did not follow that the full cost should fall on the railways. He pointed out that two passengers, each paying the same fare of, say, 7/-, could in the event of an accident receive vastly different amounts of compensation under Lord Campbell's Act. If one of the passengers was injured, he could expect to receive about £40. If the other one was killed, a jury would award a sum estimated to be the value of the passenger's life.

In the first pamphlet, as well as in the second one, which was published in 1854, there is the following description of an imaginary fatal accident to Lord Campbell, when travelling on the Kendal and Windermere Railway:

'Let us take Lord Campbell himself in illustration of his own law. It is fair, in argument, to suppose a case, which we devoutly trust will never be realised! We may imagine, therefore, that his lordship, on a tour to the Lake District, entrusts his person to the safe keeping of the Kendal and Windermere Railway. Owing to some failure of materials, or some unaccountable neglect of a pointsman or platelayer, the carriage in which his lordship is seated in solitary state, is thrown off the line and impelled over a picturesque ravine! and in a moment the judicature of the country loses an admirable Lord Chief Justice, and literature all hope of future "Lives of the Chancellors".*

'But woe to the Kendal and Windermere Company and its unfortunate shareholders if the new law shall take its course! With the salary of a Lord Chief Justice of England, enjoyed and expected to be enjoyed by his family for many years — to be consistent in carrying out the principle of this

---

*After losing the office of Lord Chancellor of Ireland, Lord Campbell wrote the *Lives of the Chancellors* — 3 series, 7 volumes, 1846/7 — a best seller.

law — the damages cannot be laid at less than ten or fifteen
thousand pounds. And, if the action succeed, the
unfortunate company is plunged into irremediable ruin.
Literally five years' dividend absorbed by an action for
damages.

'On one side of the account the hapless proprietors of the
Kendal and Windermere Railway, men who had invested
the savings of their industry, or, perhaps, their small
inheritance — the widow or the orphan who had ventured
their limited share of this world's goods in this particular
undertaking — suddenly deprived of their means of
subsistence for several years to come!

'On the other side of the account, the devisees, or
representatives, of the Lord Chief Justice obtaining by
process of an unjust law a lien or mortgage on this
important concern to the extent of £15,000, it having been
satisfactorily proved that the said Lord Chief Justice has
fulfilled his part of an assumed contract by paying some
seven shillings and sixpence for his fare, and perhaps
eighteenpence for extra luggage.'

It is of interest to mention that in the House of Lords on the
7th May 1846, when moving the third reading of the 'Death by
Accidents Compensation Bill', Lord Campbell said to the Lord
Chancellor:

'Suppose your Lordship met with an accident, how much
would a jury estimate your value to your family?'

The *Morning Chronicle* in London quoted this remark, but it
does not appear to have been reported in the Liverpool
newspapers.

In both pamphlets Henry Booth discusses the question of
limitation of liability, which was normal in all forms of
commerce, quoting the case of the maximum liability for a
horse carried by rail being £40, and suggesting that if the
liability of the railway company for a fatal accident was
limited to £100 to £200, this would be very adequate for the
ordinary passenger and that young and rising people who
might expect to earn a considerable income in the future,

could safeguard the future of their families by taking out an insurance on their lives. He pointed out that as the railway company did not know the value of the passenger, it would be very difficult for the company to insure his life. While £200 would be a very valuable sum for the dependants of the average railway passenger, and because fares had been fixed by Act of Parliament before 1846, the extra liability, under Lord Campbell's Act, was not fair.

The second pamphlet then relates the sad tale of Mr. Theophilus Jackson, a small businessman, who lived in the suburbs. His coal cellar was under the footpath adjoining his house, and unfortunately his servant forgot to replace the cover after a delivery of coal. At which juncture an eminent professional gentleman walks by, fails to see the hole in the path, falls into the cellar and is killed. The damages Mr. Jackson has to pay — £5,000 to £6,000 — completely ruin him.

The pamphlets end with an appeal to Lord Campbell to introduce an amending Act to reduce the liability on railways on the lines suggested, but there was no hope of this. Had the pamphlets been written in 1845 and 1846 and addressed to members of the House of Commons, they would have been provided with ideas as to how to amend Lord Campbell's Act when it came before them. As it was, the Commons made only one small amendment to the Bill; this was with regard to those who would be entitled to compensation.

Chapter XI

On his retirement Henry Booth was appointed a Borough Magistrate. For eight years he attended the Court with great regularity, and on his death the *Liverpool Mercury* wrote:

> 'Our local Bench of Magistrates has lost one of the most unobtrusive and yet most useful and painstaking of its members.'

Henry Booth was sitting with Mr. G.H. Lawrence on the 19th June 1860, when a man was charged with assaulting a policeman who was taking a drunk to the Bridewell. The defendant claimed that the policeman was treating his prisoner brutally. According to two cab-drivers who were called as witnesses, the defendant had only said, "Don't kill him". The defendant was found guilty and fined 2/6d. with 2/6d. costs, the Bench commenting that if the police were acting with cruelty, they would be the last people not to visit it with their disapproval. They well believed the defendant was acting from good feeling and felt that undue severity was being exercised by the officer, but that it must be borne in mind that they have a very difficult duty to perform, and, generally speaking, they conduct themselves with great moderation and propriety in such circumstances. They thought it would have been better if the defendant had noted the officer's number and brought the matter before the Court for adjudication, and not taken the almost violent part he had done.

As might have been expected, Henry Booth found the law

illogical as it was administered by the Courts, and published two pamphlets on his views. The first one, on the licensing system, deprecated the existence of Licensed Victuallers' Associations as a formidable insidious political power in the State. His view was that any fit and proper person, with suitable premises, should be entitled to obtain a licence, regardless of the objections of other licensees. He considered that charging a higher licence fee, £30 per annum, in place of £15 for public houses and £3 for beer houses, would result in more responsible licensees, reduce the number of licences, and at the same time destroy the existing monopoly. There were 1,500 public houses and 1,300 beer houses in Liverpool at this time.

Punishments were the subject of the second pamphlet; very heavy sentences being given for offences against property, compared with relatively light ones for offences against the person. Among several instances which he cited were the following:

'A prisoner, with a previous conviction, sentenced to 14 years' penal servitude for stealing 5d.'

'7 years' penal servitude for stealing a purse, three halfpence, three tickets and a postage stamp.'

'2 months' imprisonment for throwing a brickbat weighing 3 lbs at the landlord of the Waterloo Hotel, Birkenhead, breaking his nose and severely injuring his eye.'

There is a mention in Chapter II of the lecture which he gave in 1860 at the Hope Street Unitarian Church School Room on the 23rd November entitled 'The Struggle for Existence' and afterwards published as a pamphlet.* In this lecture he pointed out that the last ten years had been an epoch of general prosperity, wages had been higher and taxation had weighed less heavily than ever before on the working man. With this wonderful material prosperity, which was patent to every observer, was the condition of the labourer

*By Henry Young, 12 South Castle Street, Liverpool.

N

or artisan improved, he asked, or the number of destitute diminished. There were still overcrowded slums and excessive hours were still being worked. In the large cities, half the children were dying before they were five years old, and for a large proportion of the population there was a life of hardship and privation, and premature death. As in 1818, he believed the solution was to control the birthrate and in support of this opinion he quoted J.S. Mill's *Political Economy*. He then mentioned that everyone in Ireland was now better off, following the loss by death and emigration of two thirds of its population. It was the common idea that hardship in the great battle of life, could be overcome by good government and liberal institutions. Acts of Parliament could do little more than secure protection of life and property.

After referring to the desirability of more education, he commended to the attention of his listeners the Rochdale Co-operative Society which, by the provision of stores, corn and cotton mills, was enabling the working man to raise himself above the condition of his class. The object of his lecture was to show that the working class should be free from charity except in extremis, and that poverty should be prevented rather than relieved. He ended:

'We know how to prevent diseases such as typhus and cholera,* but in civilisation we should control numbers to the available supply of food.'

*   *   *

After his marriage in 1812 Henry Booth lived at No. 10 Lodge Lane. The house had been built for him by his father, who lived on the opposite side of the road at No. 9. When Thomas Booth died in 1832, he moved to Abercromby Square.** The

---

*In 1832 there was an outbreak of cholera in England; in Liverpool, with a population of 230,000 there were 4,912 cases and 1,523 deaths. As a result of the outbreak, the number of passengers carried by the L&MR was 74,000 less in July and August 1832 than in the previous year.
**The *Liverpool Mercury* reported on the 6th April 1832 that as a result of recent complaints from residents in Abercromby Square 'a great number of car owners had been fined 10/- each plus costs for furious driving'.

north end of Lodge Lane was close to Edge Hill and Crown Street Stations, while Abercromby Square was midway between Edge Hill and Lime Street Stations. Henry Booth's last move was to Eastbourne, Princes Park,* and after the death of her parents, their daughter Mary Anne continued to live there for a number of years.

Henry and Ellen Booth had five children, two sons and three daughters. Their elder son Henry Crompton married Marianne Trimmer; they had a son Harry, and a daughter Ellen Crompton, neither of whom appear to have married. The younger son William died unmarried at the age of 34 in 1853. Caroline, their eldest daughter, married Thomas Avison, a solicitor, and there were no children of this marriage. The second daughter, Emily, was married in 1836 to Cedric Boult, a great great uncle of Sir Adrian Boult. There do not appear to be any surviving descendants of the marriage; only one daughter married of the family of one son and five daughters.

As well as being the surviving executor of his father-in-law Abraham Crompton, Henry Booth became the sole executor of his father's will after the death of his youngest brother Charles in 1860. Thomas Booth in his last Will, made in 1824, had appointed as his executors, his four sons who were living in Liverpool. His estate was to be held in trust and not wound up until the death of his last surviving daughter. The income and the residual estate were to be divided equally amongst those of his children or grandchildren alive on his death. The estate had been administered by Thomas Booth & Company from 1832 until 1853 and then by Charles until his death. Thomas Booth's son James, went to Trinity College, Cambridge and became a barrister in London. In 1839 he was appointed Counsel to the Speaker of the House of Commons, being responsible for an improved form in the preparation of Bills, and he was made Permanent Secretary to the Board of Trade in 1850. From there he wrote the following letter to his brother:

'Acknowledgement of £150 Dividend Cheque on Barclay

---

*Now No. 12 Sefton Park Road and called 'The Vice-Chancellor's Lodge'.

Feb 27 63

My Dear Henry

Many thanks for your letter & its welcome inclosure. The first "quarter" of the year is a heavy one and none of my securities pay their Interest in that quarter so that a windfall is particularly acceptable.

Jane* has been ailing a good deal of late and for a long time & we are in great hopes that an arsenical paper in the Bed room may have something to do with it. We are having it routed out & I hope things will go better.

What a rhetorician Seward** is — I think things are coming to a crisis —

Love to you all
Ever afft yrs
James Booth'

The interest of this letter is the reference in it to 'arsenical paper'. At that time arsenic had often been made the scapegoat when an illness could not be diagnosed.

After the death of Henry Booth, his son-in-law Thomas Avison administered Thomas Booth's estate, which was not wound up until 1872 on the death of Esther Booth, his last surviving daughter.

In her diary for 1868 Charles Booth's youngest daughter Hester Emily Booth (1842-1905) wrote:

'On the 1st Feb. Mr. [William] Rathbone died. All the week before Uncle Booth had been very ill but he got better for the time.'

Henry Booth made his last Will in 1865, adding a second Codicil on the 11th September 1868. He had originally directed his Trustees, Thomas and Caroline Avison and Mary Anne Booth, to pay his wife an annuity of £600 during her lifetime. According to the second Codicil:

'Whereas the mental capacity of my wife has become

---

*His wife, Jane née Noble, a cousin.
**William Seward — Secretary of State in Abraham Lincoln's Administration.

enfeebled in so much that it would be inexpedient in any case to pay the said annuity direct . . . the annuity be paid to my daughter Mary Anne (who has long been associated with me in the charge of her mother) to be applied as she may deem expedient. . . .'

Originally all the furniture, plate, books and pictures were to be partitioned amongst his children; the Codicil directed that:

'In consideration of my daughter Mary Anne having been left for many years alone with her parents whose age and infirmities have increased and may be expected still to increase while life remains . . . I direct that my daughter Mary Anne may appropriate to herself as a free gift such portions of the household furniture . . . glass china books prints pictures . . . as she may desire.'

Hester Emily writes in her diary for 1869 of the christening of her nephew Charles on the 2nd January and that 'Uncle Booth' was among those present. A later entry records that:

'Uncle Booth who had been failing for more than a year grew much worse in March, and died at the end of the month.'

Henry Booth died on the 28th March. His funeral was on Thursday, the 1st April at the Ancient Chapel of Toxteth; the Minister of Renshaw Street Chapel, the Rev. C. Beard, officiated at the service. His grave is on the east side of the Chapel. A memorial tablet was put up in the Renshaw Street Chapel; it is now in the Ullet Road Unitarian Church, to which the congregation of the Renshaw Street Chapel moved in 1899.

The obituaries of Henry Booth in the newspapers covered the main work and interest of his life — railways — and his involvement in various matters concerning the community. The following excerpt from the [*Liverpool*] *Daily Post* has been chosen, as from it emerges a clear picture of the man and, in some respects, of other descendants of Thomas Booth:

'. . . and great as his personal and intellectual merits were, he lacked one element necessary to social enlargement — he was not a genial man. Although not addicted to conversation, and prone somewhat to silence, he had acquired a habit of indulging in sarcasm, but his sarcasms lacked the advantage of wit; but not withstanding his offence in that direction, it never made him an enemy, although they were very personal . . . .

'For a gentleman so thoughtful, so useful in his sphere of life, and so beneficial to the world at large, he was never considered a remarkable man. That was owing principally to his retiring disposition and the want of that easy kind of sauvity which converts all who approach into friends.'

At the end of the *Memoir* by Robert Smiles there is a letter from W.B.H. a personal friend of Henry Booth for many years, and the following extracts are from this letter:

'. . . Mr. Booth was not a man easily to be known. He did not "wear his heart upon his sleeve" . . . . He was a grave, reserved, reticent, somewhat even stern man, more given to listening than to talking . . . . The long and constant habit of dealing with interests of vast complexity and importance, the weight of responsibility ever resting upon him . . . only steadied and strengthened him . . . .

'We, who accept with as little gratitude as wonder the marvellous results of our railway system — who complain of the slightest delay or inconvenience . . . find it difficult . . . to realize the enormous difficulties of the first beginning and the early progress, and the amount of forethought needed in anticipation of all experience, not merely to organize, but to adapt to ever-shifting exigencies, and to provide for the rapid growth of an organization which developed itself simultaneously on so many sides . . . . In this gigantic work, of which the issues only were apparent . . . the main agent throughout was really Mr. Booth; and though to the public generally his name has not yet been so familiar as that of some others, his merit has been frankly recognized by those whose position gave them a knowledge of the facts.

'By those who knew him intimately he was most beloved; respected and trusted by all, it was in the friendly, and, still more, in the domestic circle that his real excellence was best to be discerned. Above all things, he was a just and truthful man . . . .

'With his experience and power of thought, it would have been a strange anomaly had he not been a zealous advocate of popular education. Not, however, in the sense of making the multitude acquainted with bare reading or writing . . . but in order to develop in every one for the world's gain as well as his own whatever faculty might be within him, and to urge and to guide and to qualify every one for the discharge of the duties of this life, beginning with the first duty of self-support by honest industry and prudent self-control.

'His religion was, like himself, simple, sincere, earnest, practical . . . . It was once remarked . . . of one who made no religious profession, that he had no religion to speak of. When this remark was reported to him he said calmly, "It is true; I have no religion — to speak of." So with Mr. Booth, religion was a thing not to speak of, but to live by.'

On the 1st April 1869, the day of Henry Booth's funeral, the L&NWR opened its direct line to Crewe, crossing the Mersey at Runcorn, a line first proposed more than forty years previously. The journey time to London was reduced to 5¼ hours, but although the distance was 9 miles less, fares remained the same.

A statue of Henry Booth, with a replica of his double screw coupling held in the left hand, was later erected outside St. George's Hall, Liverpool. The statue is now at the top of the stairs inside the north entrance in William Brown Street.

One of the L&NWR Precedent class 2-4-0 engines, introduced in 1874 — No. 308 — was given the name Booth.

Precedent class locomotive

Appendix I

Railway Office, Liverpool,
25th April, 1829.

STIPULATIONS AND CONDITIONS

On which the Directors of the Liverpool and Manchester Railway offer a Premium of £500 for the most improved Locomotive Engine.

1st.—The said Engine must "effectually consume its own smoke," according to the provisions of the Railway Act, 7th Geo. IV.

2d.—The Engine, if it weighs Six Tons, must be capable of drawing after it, day by day, on a well-constructed Railway, on a level plane, a Train of Carriages of the gross weight of Twenty Tons, including the Tender and Water Tank, at the rate of Ten Miles per Hour, with a pressure of steam in the boiler not exceeding 50lb on the square inch.

3d.—There must be two Safety Valves, one of which must be completely out of the reach or control of the Engine-man, and neither of which must be fastened down while the Engine is working.

4th.—The Engine and Boiler must be supported on Springs, and rest on Six Wheels; and the height, from the ground to the top of the Chimney, must not exceed Fifteen Feet.

5th.—The weight of the Machine, *with its complement of water* in the Boiler, must, at most, not exceed Six Tons; and a Machine of less weight will be preferred if it draw *after* it a *proportionate* weight; and if the weight of the Engine, &c. do not exceed *Five Tons,* then the gross weight to be drawn need not exceed Fifteen Tons; and in that proportion for Machines of still smaller weight—provided that the Engine, &c. shall still be on six wheels, unless the weight (as above) be reduced to Four Tons and a Half, or under, in which case the Boiler, &c. may be placed on four wheels. And the Company shall be at liberty to put the Boiler, Fire Tube, Cylinders, &c. to the test of a pressure of water not exceeding 150lb per square inch, without being answerable for any damage the Machine may receive in consequence.

6th—There must be a Mercurial Gauge affixed to the Machine, with Index Rod, showing the Steam Pressure above 45 pounds per square inch; and constructed to blow out at a pressure of 60 pounds per inch.

7th.—The Engine to be delivered complete for trial, at the Liverpool end of the Railway, not later than the 1st of October next.

8th.—The price of the Engine, which may be accepted, not to exceed £550, delivered on the Railway; and any Engine not approved to be taken back by the Owner.

N.B.—The Railway Company will provide the *Engine Tender* with a supply of Water and Fuel, for the experiment. The distance within the rails is four feet eight inches and a half.

Appendix II

Newcastle-upon-Tyne,
August 3rd, 1829.

My Dear Sir,

Since my arrival arrangements have been made which I expect will enable us to have the premium engine working in the factory say this day three weeks. This will give us time to make experiments or any alterations that may suggest themselves. The tubes are nearly all made, the whole number will be completed by to-morrow night, they are an excellent job. The only point I consider at all doubtful is the clinking of the ends of the tubes. The body of the boiler is finished, and is a good piece of workmanship. The cylinder and other parts of the engine are in a forward state. After weighing such parts as are in progress, the following is an estimate of their weights:

	CWT.	QRS.	LBS.
Boiler, without the tubes	9	3	7
25 copper tubes	4	2	22
Frames, carriages and bolts	4	3	3
1 pair of 4 ft. 8½ in. wheels and axle	13	1	0
1 pair of wagon wheels and axle	5	0	0
4 springs and bolts	2	0	20
Copper fire-place, including bars, etc.	6	0	0
Chimney and soot	2	0	0
4 supports for boiler on frame	1	2	4
2 engines complete, each 8 cwt.	16	0	0
Water in train boiler	11	3	0
Water in copper fire-box	3	0	0
	80	0	0

This weight, I believe, will cover everything. The wheels I am arranging so as to throw 2½ tons upon the large wheels in order to get friction upon the rail. *Will there be any fatal objection raised to this?* You had better get the tender made in Liverpool; the coach makers that made the last tender will make one neater than our men. The barrel might be covered with something like the body of a coach. It may be made lighter than the last.

We are daily expecting the arrival of the fire-box. I hope you will despatch it as quickly as possible, as we shall require it in 4 or 5 days. I have heard from Dixon that the iron hoops are failing upon the locomotives at that end of the line. Supposing that you would require spare wheels, I have ordered 4 metal ones to be got ready immediately; if you do not mean to have any spare ones, they can be used elsewhere. I thought it might be useful to have them ready. I am apprehensive that wooden wheels will be abandoned; a pair of them failed at Darlington some time ago — on the common wagons they appear to stand well.

The failure of the hoop on travelling engines I am inclined to attribute to the horizontal connecting-rods, confining the wheels, when partially and unequally worn, to revolve in the same time, whilst the circumferences are unequal. This, indeed, appears the only distinction between the two applications. In the small engine the objection will not exist, and I am further persuaded a considerable loss of power is to be ascribed to this defect.

Yours most respectfully,

(*Signed*) Rob. Stephenson.

I will write you in a few days detailing Hackworth's plan of boiler; it is ingenious, but it will not destroy the smoke with coal, which I understand is intended to form a portion of this fuel; coke will be the remainder — he does not appear to understand that a coke fire will only burn briskly when the escape of the carbonic acid gas is immediate. If the two large wheels having 2½ tons upon them is an objection, please inform me. Some reduction may perhaps be made, but it must be very little, or the friction upon the rail will be inadequate to the load assigned.

*

Newcastle-upon-Tyne,
August 21st, 1829.

My Dear Sir,

Having been a good deal from home since I wrote you last, I

have not had an opportunity of writing you particulars of our progress so promptly as I promised. The tubes are all clunk into the boiler, which is placed on the frame; wheels, springs and axle-carriages are all finished. The clinking of the tubes is tight with boiling water. I am arranging the hydraulic pump to prove the boiler up to 160 lbs. before proceeding any further. The cylinder and working gear is very neatly finished. I expect the mode for changing the gear will please you; it is now as simple as I can make it, and I believe effectual. The fire-box is put in its place, but it is not quite square built, which gives rise to a little apparent neglect in the workmanship; I have endeavoured to hide it as much as possible. To-morrow week I expect we shall be ready for trial in the evening.

I should like to see you at Newcastle on the following Monday to make further trial, so that we might consult respecting any alterations that may suggest themselves during trial. I will write you between now and then to say positively when we shall make the trial, in the meantime let me know if you could get away from Liverpool. My father may perhaps also come, although he had better not be pressed for fear of something happening in his absence. . . . Please inform my father and Mr. Locke the progress we have made. Could you, without inconvenience, procure us any money on account of the locomotive last sent — if you could do so I should feel particularly obliged — the price is £550. Hoping to hear from you to say if I may expect the pleasure of seeing you at Newcastle.

I am, Yours faithfully,

(*Signed*) Robt. Stephenson.

*

Newcastle-on-Tyne,
August 26th, 1829.

My Dear Sir,

On Wednesday I had the boiler filled with water and put up the pressure of 70 lbs. per square inch, when I found that the yielding of the boiler end injured the clinking of the tubes. I therefore thought it prudent to stop the experiment until we got some stays put into the boiler longitudinally. The boiler end at 70 lbs. per square inch came out full $^3/_{16}$ths of an inch. This, you may easily conceive, put a serious strain on the clinking at the tube end. To-day I had the pressure up to a little above 70, the tubes were nearly every one tight, but the deflection of the end still was more than it was prudent to pass over. I am, therefore, putting in five more stays, which I believe will be effectual. A circumstance which has occurred within a few days induces me to regard severe pressures upon boilers injudicious. We put up two hydraulic presses in a paper mill, which are to bear 6½ tons per square inch — the pipes which lead to the presses from the pumps were proved up to the pressure previous to leaving the factory and continued to act well for a week, when they burst with 5 tons per square inch. A new set of pipes were made which withstood the proof pressure, but afterwards burst with much less pressure. Query: Therefore, is it judicious to prove the boilers to 150 lbs. per square inch? I should say not. A pressure of 100 lbs. per square inch would not be objectionable. If the engines were not so limited in weight, then I would say prove them to 150 lbs. or more. The chimney is made 14 inches diameter, being a little less than the area of the horizontal tubes. I think it should be less, the air being cooler it consequently occupied less space in the chimney than in the tubes. I am still sanguine as regards the weight — 4 tons, I believe, will cover all. Of course I am calculating that if the engine is reduced in weight below 4½, the last load dragged will be reduced in the same proportion. I am much pleased to hear of the performance of the *Lancashire Witch*; the more I hear, and experience I have in the locomotive principle, the more thoroughly I am convinced of its convenient adaptation to public railways. The putting in of the stays will delay the trial of the engine until Tuesday. If anything unexpected starts up I will let you know.

Yours faithfully,

(*Signed*) Robt. Stephenson.

The wheels are made 4 ft. 8½ in. — the small pair 2 ft. 6 in.

*

Newcastle,
August 31st, 1829.

My Dear Sir,

After the stays were put in we tried the boiler up to 120 lbs. per square inch, when I found it necessary to put in two more stays in order to make the ends withstand 150. This would be totally unnecessary if the fixed pressure for trial were 120. We can, however, make it stand the required pressure, although I scarcely think it prudent from what I stated in my last. The putting in of these stays has put the trial of the engine off until Wednesday. The mercurial gauge is nearly finished, it will look well — the pipes being of wrought iron have taken more time than I expected. The wheels of the engine are painted in the same manner as coach wheels, and look extremely well. The same character of painting I intend keeping up throughout the engine, it will look light, which is one object we ought to aim at. Mr. Burstall, junior, is in Newcastle, I have little doubt for the purpose of getting information. I was extremely mystified to find that he walked into the manufactory the morning and examined the engine, with all the coolness imaginable, before we discovered who he was. He has, however, scarcely time to take advantage of any hints he might catch during his transient visit. It would have been as well if he had not seen anything. I will write you on Wednesday evening or Thursday morning.

Your faithfully,
(*Signed*) Robt. Stephenson.

*

Newcastle-on-Tyne,
September 5th, 1829.

Dear Sir,

I daresay you are getting anxious, but I have delayed writing you until I tried the engine on Killingworth Railway. It appeared prudent to make an actual trial and make any alterations that might present themselves during an experiment of that kind. The fire burns admirably, and abundance of steam is raised when the fire is carefully attended to. This is an essential point because a coke fire when let down is bad to get up again; this rather prevented our experiment being so successful as it would have been throughout. We also found, from the construction of the working gear, that the engine did not work so well in one direction as in the other. This will be remedied. The mercurial gauge was not on, not from any defect, but from my wish to get the engine tried. We started from Killingworth Pit with five wagons, each weighing 4 tons. Add to this the tender and 40 men, we proceeded up an ascent of 11 or 12 feet per mile at 8 miles per hour after we had fairly gained our speed. We went 3 miles on this railway, the scale of ascents and descents my father knows — on a level part laid with malleable iron rails we attained a speed of 12 miles per hour, and without thinking that I deceived myself (I tried to avoid this), I believe the steam did not sink on this part. On the whole, the engine is capable of doing as much, if not more, than set forth in the stipulations. After a great deal of trouble and anxiety we have got the tubes perfectly tight. As requested by you in Mr. Locke's letter, I have not tried the boiler above 120 lbs. The mercurial gauge and some other knickknacks are yet to be put on. On Friday next the engine will leave by way of Carlisle, and will arrive in Liverpool on Wednesday week.

I am, dear Sir,
Yours faithfully,
(*Signed*) Robt. Stephenson.

Appendix III

TRIAL OF THE LOCOMOTIVE ENGINES.

LIVERPOOL & MANCHESTER
RAIL WAY.

The following is the Ordeal which we have decided each Locomotive Engine shall undergo, in contending for the Premium of £500, at Rainhill.

The weight of the Locomotive Engine, with its full compliment of water in the boiler, shall be ascertained at the Weighing Machine, by eight o'clock in the morning, and the load assigned to it, shall be three times the weight thereof. The water in the boiler shall be cold, and there shall be no fuel in the fire-place. As much fuel shall be weighed, and as much water shall be measured and delivered into the Tender Carriage, as the owner of the Engine may consider sufficient for the supply of the Engine for a journey of thirty-five miles. The fire in the boiler shall then be lighted, and the quantity of fuel consumed for getting up the steam shall be determined, and the time noted.

The Tender Carriage, with the fuel and water, shall be considered to be, and taken as part of the load assigned to the engine.

Those Engines that carry their own fuel and water, shall be allowed a proportionate deduction from their load, according to the weight of the engine.

The Engine, with the Carriages attached to it, shall be run by hand up to the Starting Post, and as soon as the steam is got up to fifty pounds per square inch, the engine shall set out upon its journey.

The distance the Engine shall perform each trip, shall be one mile and three quarters each way, including one-eighth of a mile at each end for getting up the speed, and for stopping the train, by this means the engine with its load, will travel one and a half mile each way at full speed

The Engine shall make ten trips, which will be equal to a journey of thirty-five miles, thirty miles whereof shall be performed at full speed, and the average rate of travelling shall not be less than ten miles per hour.

As soon as the Engine has performed this task, which will be equal to the travelling from Liverpool to Manchester, there shall be a fresh supply of fuel and water delivered to her, and as soon as she can be got ready to set out again, she shall go up to the Starting Post and make ten trips more, which will be equal to the journey from Manchester back again to Liverpool.

The time of performing every trip shall be accurately noted, as well as the time occupied in getting ready to set out on the second journey.

Should the Engine not be enabled to take along with it sufficient fuel and water for the journey of ten trips, the time occupied in taking in a fresh supply of fuel and water, and shall be considered and taken as part of the time in performing the journey.

J. U. RASTRICK, Esq. Stourbridge, C. E.
NICHOLAS WOOD, Esq. Killingworth, C. E. } Judges.
JOHN KENNEDY, Esq. Manchester,

Liverpool, Oct. 6, 1829.

Appendix IV

WHISHAW'S PRACTICAL
LOCOMOTIVE EXPERIMENTS

Whishaw used a special watch graduated to 1/100 of a minute, but the maximum speeds, which he records, are suspect. The speeds on a few of his journeys are given in graphs; on the Grand Junction Railway, where the distance posts used for timing were at 100 yard intervals, they fluctuate violently. In two trips, where he claimed maximum speeds of 68.18 m.p.h. down Madely Bank, between Stafford and Crewe, the sequences of readings are:

40/48/45/37/34/68/45/47/50/25/27

37/42/50/57/29/35/68/49/68/35/35/30/42/42/42/57/42

Apart from some posts not being correctly sited, there must have been errors in reading and recording the times.

On the L&NR, where the posts were at ¼ mile intervals, only one journey (No. 6 in the table) is shown as a graph. Here a maximum of 50 m.p.h. was claimed on a slightly falling gradient, after passing St. Helens Junction at the foot of Sutton Incline. From that point the sequence of speeds were:

35/30/50/41/32½/30/33

It is probable that the maximum speeds on the L&MR never exceeded 40 m.p.h., and on the Grand Junction 45 to 48 m.p.h.

Notes on the Tables
Suspect maximum speeds are shown in brackets.
All the engines used were 2-2-2, with 5 ft. diameter driving wheels. Roderic and Rokeby had 11" by 18" cylinders, the others 14" by 12".

o

Table I

Edge Hill to Newton 14¼ miles

Run No:	6	8	10	21	25	
Date November:	11	11	11	27	28	
Engine	Milo	Arrow	Ròderic	Roderic	Roderic	
Load Gross	22½	27	24	28	28½	tons
Vehicles	5	6	6	7	7	
Train ex Lime Street	8.45 am	11.0 am	2.0 pm	8.45 am	8.45 am	
Left Edge Hill	8.53	11.14	2.03	8.56	9.06	
Time to Newton	29½	30	32	38½*	33	minutes
Stops	1	-	1	-	-	
Nett time to Newton	28	30	30½	38½	33	minutes
Average speed	30½	28½	28	22	26	m.p.h.
Maximum speed	(50)	35	(44)	34	36	m.p.h.
Speeds on Whiston Incline						
Foot	36	30½	25	23	28¼	m.p.h.
Top	24	20¼	25	14	18½	m.p.h.

*Head winds were the cause of the low speed on this run.

Table II

Newton to Edge Hill 14¼ miles

Run No:	7	9	11	
All made on 11th November				
Engine	Rokeby	Vesuvius	Arrow	
Load Gross	32½	23½	35	tons
Vehicles	8	6	10	
Train ex Manchester	9.0 am	11.45 am*	2.45 pm*	
Left Newton	9.49	12.40	3.46	
Time to Edge Hill	41¼	48½	52	minutes
Stops	-	7	7	
Nett time to Edge Hill	41¼	41½	43	minutes
Average speed	20½	20	20	m.p.h.
Maximum speed	(47)	33½	(40½)	m.p.h.
Speed on Sutton Incline				
Foot	14½	21½	17½	m.p.h.
Top	(B) 22	9	(B) 22	m.p.h.

(B) Banked up incline; run No: 7. Banker Buffalo 0 - 4 - 2. 14" by 20" cylinders.
*2nd class Blue Trains.

Table III

Edge Hill to Manchester		29¼ miles	Manchester to Edge Hill		
Run No:	17	28	5	18	
Date:	25/11	2/12	9/11	25/11	1839
Engine	Rokeby	Panther	Milo	Comet	

Load gross (Tons) 15¼ 18½ 39 30½ to Kenyon Jct.
                                      22½ on
Vehicles 4 5 9 7 to Kenyon Jct.
                          5 on
Train ex Lime Street 10.0 am* 11.45 am* 7.0 pm 5.0 pm(M) ex
                                                    Manchester

Left Edge Hill	10.18	11.54	7.25	5.04	
Time on journey	101	98½	87¼	70¾	minutes
Stops	16	12	3	2	
Nett time on journey	86	86¼	83½	68½	minutes

Speeds on Whiston Incline
Foot 16 25½ m.p.h. No record of speeds
Top 16 21 m.p.h. as after nightfall
Average speed 20½ 20½ 21 25½ m.p.h.
Maximum speed (43) (40½) m.p.h.

*2nd class Blue Trains.
(M) Mixed 1st and 2nd class train.

Appendix V

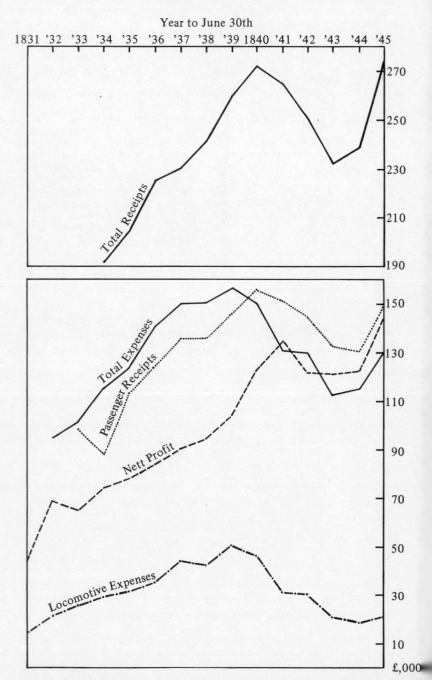

Appendix VI

Letter from Charles Lawrence, Esq. *to* Mr. Booth.

Mosley Hill, Liverpool, 12th Oct., 1846.

My Dear Sir,

After having witnessed your valuable services, and profited by your assistance for above twenty years, it is a matter of extreme gratification to me, to be the medium of conveying to you the accompanying Resolution of a numerous and highly respectable body of Railway Proprietors, confirmatory of their sense of your long and arduous exertions in favor of that most stupendous of modern inventions, which has occupied for some years so much of the attention of both Europe and America.

Acting on the present occasion for Gentlemen interested in different Railways, it would not become me to dilate too much upon that particular concern which brought me more intimately into communication with you; or to express all I feel of my own individual sense of obligation to you, — but when I reflect, that the Railway I allude to was the pioneer of all Lines, made, or now making, I should not be justified in neglecting to record that fact, any more than in failing to testify what advantages have been derived from the admirable judgment and unwearied assiduity with which you assisted to organise that first Railway, from which, I believe, all succeeding ones have so materially profited.

I have now only to add, that I am instructed to request your acceptance of the Plate, which Messrs. Jones and Sons will send you, and the inclosed Order on the Bank for the balance, from our Honorary Treasurer, Mr. H. Earle; and that

I am,

My dear Sir,

With great esteem and cordiality,

Yours truly,

Charles Lawrence.

Henry Booth, Esq.

Mr. Booth *to* Charles Lawrence, Esq.

Liverpool, 19th October, 1846.

My Dear Sir,

I have very great pleasure in acknowledging your esteemed communication of the 12th instant, presenting me with the liberal and handsome Testimonial, which the kindness of many friends has offered to my acceptance. The present moment may well be considered an epoch of my life, now, that the events of the last twenty years crowd in review before me — hurriedly and imperfectly, but with an iron outline, that will not easily be effaced from my mind.

The introduction of Railways, as you observe, has not been limited to this Country; Europe and America and the two Indies claim part in those influences, which have already impressed themselves on the character and views of society, stimulating the industry, exciting the energies, and adding to the capabilities of all classes of the community. The extended intercourse between individuals, and towns, and nations, has yet only partially produced its fruits. The Locomotive Engine must not alone be regarded as the mechanical wonder of the age, but in concert with its great co-adjutor the Steam Ship, is destined, I trust, to do good service in promoting commerce, peace, and civilization, throughout the world.

To have taken a prominent part in originating this great movement, may fairly be considered a subject of mutual congratulation. In the list of my friends on this occasion, I see, with pleasure, many of the early supporters of the Liverpool and Manchester Railway — that type and forerunner of a hundred others. Fortunate for me, that from my official connexion with the first great work of the kind, it was my province to give effect to the deliberations and decisions of Directors, who in former days, through evil report and good report, without favor from the Legislature, or encouragement from the Public, while the risk was evident, and the gain problematical, with intelligence, perseverance, and singleness of purpose, pursued their work, till success crowned their labors, and multitudes were eager to follow in their steps.

The old Liverpool and Manchester Railway, in name and title, exists no longer — being connected, now, with other

Lines, and forming but one link in the chain, which unites Liverpool and Manchester with London. The first Railway may be said, already, to be matter of history; but its promoters having completed their work, have not forgotten the humble Individual, who so long labored for them and with them. Most devoutly do I wish that I had better earned this mark of their favor; but conscious that lack of zeal and good intent has seldom been amongst my failings, I can almost derive satisfaction from the thought, that the more frequent my short comings, in times past, the greater their kindness on this occasion.

In returning you my best acknowledgments, I address you as the representative of those numerous friends, in various parts of the Kingdom, who have contributed to this bounty. To you, individually, for twenty years Chairman of the First Railway, I may be allowed to refer to the high gratification I have experienced personally from your unvaried kindness and support, in an uninterrupted intercourse for that long period. To them and to you I wish I could more worthily express the grateful sentiments with which I accept this liberal Testimonial at your hands.

I remain,

My dear Sir,

Very sincerely, your obliged,

Henry Booth.

To Charles Lawrence, Esq., Mosley Hill.

The following is a Copy of the Inscription on the Base of the Candelabrum:

PRESENTED,

WITH A

PURSE OF TWO THOUSAND EIGHT HUNDRED GUINEAS,

BY A LARGE BODY OF RAILWAY PROPRIETORS, TO

HENRY BOOTH, Esq.

TREASURER AND CHIEF MANAGER

OF

THE LIVERPOOL AND MANCHESTER RAILWAY

FOR A PERIOD OF TWENTY YEARS,

AS A

GRATEFUL ACKNOWLEDGMENT

OF HIS VALUABLE SERVICES TO THE RAILWAY INTEREST

IN THE

SUCCESSFUL ADAPTATION TO THE WANTS OF THE PUBLIC OF A

NEW SYSTEM OF INTERNAL COMMUNICATION, BY WHICH

THE EARLY PROJECTORS OF RAILWAYS OBTAINED

THE JUST REWARD OF THEIR ENTERPRISE,

AND THEIR SUCCESSORS,

THE BENEFIT OF EXPERIENCE, WITHOUT ITS COST.

MDCCCXLVI.

Index

(*People*)

Index

(*Places and Things*)

P

Bibliography

NINETEENTH CENTURY

Baines, T.
  History of the Commerce and Town of Liverpool   1852

Cooke, C.J. Bowen
  British Locomotives   1893
    (Re-printed 1979)

Fletcher, Thomas
  Autobiographical Memoirs   1843

Francis, J.
  A History of the English Railway   1851

Head, F.B.
  Stokers and Pokers   1849
    (Re-printed 1968)

Jeffreson, J.C.
  Life of Robert Stephenson   1864

de Pambour, Comte F.M.G.
  A Practical Treatise on Locomotives   1838

Rastrick, J.V.
  Report to the Directors on the Comparative Merits   1829
  of Locomotives and Fixed Engines

Smiles, Robert
  Memoir of the late Henry Booth   1869

Smiles, Samuel
  Life of George Stephenson   1857
  Lives of the Engineers   1868

Stephenson, R. and Locke, J.
  Observations on the Comparative Merits   1830
  of Locomotives and Fixed Engines

Sylvester, C.
  Report on Rail Roads and Locomotive Engines   1825

Tredgold, T.
  On the Steam Engine   1838

Whishaw, F.
  The Railways of Great Britain and Ireland   1840

Wood, Nicholas
  A Practical Treatise on Railroads   1838
    (3rd Edition)

PERIODICALS
   Edinburgh Review   October 1832
   Mechanic's Magazine   June 1829 - 1837
   (Railway Magazine   1835 - 1851
   (Herapath's Railway
   (*Magazine* and various similar titles

NEWSPAPERS
   Liverpool Mercury
   The Albion
   Liverpool Courier
   Liverpool Journal
   Liverpool Times and Billinge's Advertiser
   Gore's General Advertiser
   (Liverpool) Daily Post
   Manchester Guardian

TWENTIETH CENTURY
Ahrons, E.L.
   The British Steam Locomotive   1925
Carlson, R.E.
   The Liverpool and Manchester Railway Project   1969
   1821 - 1831
Donaghy, T.J.
   Liverpool and Manchester Railway Operation   1972
   1831 - 1845
Holt, Anne
   Walking Together   1938
Holt, G.O.
   A Short History of the Liverpool and Manchester   1955
   Railway
Marshall, C. Dendy
   Two Essays in Early Locomotive History   1928
   Centenary History of the Liverpool and   1930
   Manchester Railway
Muir, Ramsay
   History of Municipal Government in Liverpool   1906
Neele, G.P.
   Neele's Notes of a Railway Superintendant's Life   1904
Nock, O.S.
   The London and North Western Railway   1960

Potter, **Beatrix**
   The Journal of Beatrix Potter 1881 - 1897   1966
Rolt, L.T.C.
   George and Robert Stephenson   1964
Singleton, D.
   The Liverpool and Manchester Railway   1975
   (*Mile by Mile Guide*)
Steel, W.L.
   History of the London and North Western Railway   1914
Thomas, R.H.G.
   The Liverpool & Manchester Railway   1979
Tuplin, W.A.
   Steam Locomotives   1975
Veitch, G.S.
   The Struggle for the Liverpool and   1930
   Manchester Railway
Warren, J.G.H.
   A Century of Locomotive Building   1923
                      (Re-printed 1970)

Whitting, **Harriet Anna**
   Alfred Booth   1917
Young, R.
   Timothy Hackworth and the Locomotive   1923

Consulted

P.R.O. DOCUMENTS
L&MR
   Directors' Minutes   1826 - 1845
   Finance Committee Minutes   1824 - 1831
   Management/Sub-Committee Minutes   1831 - 1845
   General Meetings Minutes   1826 - 1845
   Reports   1826 - 1845
             (some missing — 1828/9 in WBL)
Reports on Accident to Patentee   1836
   Report by G. Stephenson on Fixed and Locomotive   1828
      Engines (also contains copies of R. Stephenson's
      letters to Henry Booth re the Rocket)
L&BR
   Board Minutes   1837/9
   Secretary's Letters

GJR
    Board (Local) Minutes   1845 - 1851
    Reports
L&NWR
    Board Minutes   1845 - 1859
    Court of Proprietors Minutes and Reports   1845 - 1859
    Mr. Booth's Report   1848 - 1850
    Mr. Booth's Report on Permanent Way   1855
    Other Reports to Board   1852 - 1858
    Letters — Henry Booth to Leeds and   1849
       Dewsbury Railway
    Crewe Committee Minutes   1846 - 1855
    General Locomotive Committee   1846 - 1858
    Northern Locomotive Sub-Committee   1852 - 1858
    Northern Sub-Committee Liverpool   1852 - 1850
    Letters of Sir Richard Moon   1855 - 1858

Leeds & Dewsbury Railway   )
Huddersfield & Manchester Railway   ) Directors'   1848/9
Manchester South Junction & Altrincham) Minutes
    Railway   )

Dictionary of National Biography

Wills — Abraham Crompton
       Thomas Booth
       Lucy Crompton
       Henry Booth
       Mary Anne Booth

Henry Booth's Publications

1813 *Moral Capability* (Lecture)

1818 (GL) *The Question of the Poor Laws*

1830 *An Account of the Liverpool & Manchester Railway*
      (Re-printed 1969)

1833 *Free Trade as it Affects the People addressed to a*
      Reformed Parliament

1839 (WBL) *Observations on the Force of the Wind and the*
      Resistance of the Air (Lecture)

1841 (GL) *The Carrying Question and Railway Passenger*
      Duty
      (On the L&BR 15 carriers share the goods traffic at
      Camden Town; a wasteful and expensive survival of
      canal traffic. The L&MR and GJR do not use them.
      The present scale of tax on railway passengers —
      1/8 d. per mile — excessive on 3rd. class fares. A
      sliding scale from 10% to 2½% on lowest fares
      suggested.)

1847 *The Rationale of the Currency Question*

1852 *The Case of the Railways . . . and the Operation of*
      Lord Campbell's Act

1853 *Master and Man*

1854 *A Letter to Lord Campbell*

1860 *The Struggle for Existence*

Mentioned by Robert Smiles Copies untraced

1847 *Uniformity of Time*

1857 *Approaches to St. George's Hall* (Letter to Francis
      Shand — Mayor)
      (Henry Booth was on the Building Committee of St.
      George's Hall)

1860 *Taxation Direct and Indirect*
      (Because personal allowances for income tax payers
      were unknown, direct taxes would be as grave a
      burden as indirect; the ability of the wealthy to give
      employment made direct taxes undesirable.)

1862 *Consideration on the Licensing Question*

1863   *The Question of Comparative Punishments*
     (and — *Atlantic Steam Navigation* — described by
     Smiles as 'a clever brochure')

Responsible for:
1832   (WBL) Answer of Directors to an article in the
     Edinburgh Review
1836   (GL) Letter to H.M. Commissioners on Railways in
     Ireland

     Copies in British Library except where otherwise
     stated
     GL   The Goldsmiths' Library, University of London
     WBL William Brown Library, Liverpool

Genealogies of the Booths and Cromptons

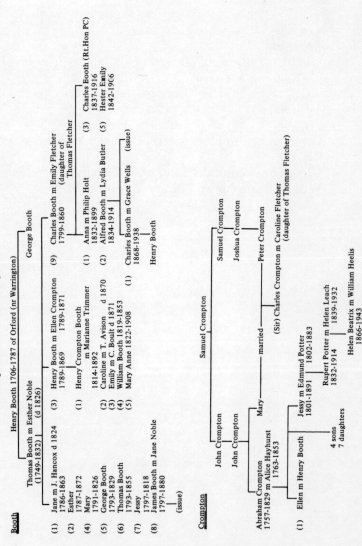

Booth

Henry Booth 1706-1787 of Orford (nr Warrington)

Thomas Booth m Esther Noble
(1749-1832) | (d 1826)

George Booth

(1) Jane m J. Hancox d 1824
    1786-1863

(2) Esther
    1787-1872

(4) Mary
    1791-1826

(5) George Booth
    1793-1829

(6) Thomas Booth
    1793-1855

(7) Jessy
    1797-1818

(8) James Booth m Jane Noble
    1797-1880

    (issue)

(3) Henry Booth m Ellen Crompton
    1789-1869   1789-1871

(1) Henry Crompton Booth
    m Marianne Trimmer
    1814-1892

(2) Caroline m T. Avison   d 1870

(3) Emily m C. Boult d 1871

(4) William Booth 1819-1853

(5) Mary Anne 1822-1908   (1)

(9) Charles Booth m Emily Fletcher
    1799-1860   (daughter of
                      Thomas Fletcher

(1) Anna m Philip Holt   (3) Charles Booth (Rt.Hon PC)
    1832-1899   1837-1916

(2) Alfred Booth m Lydia Butler (5) Hester Emily
    1834-1914   1842-1906

    Charles Booth m Grace Wells   (issue)
    1868-1938

    Henry Booth

Crompton

Samuel Crompton

John Crompton

John Crompton

Mary

Samuel Crompton

Joshua Crompton

Peter Crompton

married   (Sir) Charles Crompton m Caroline Fletcher
                                        (daughter of Thomas Fletcher)

Abraham Crompton
1757-1829 m Alice Hayhurst
          1763-1853

(1) Ellen m Henry Booth

    4 sons
    7 daughters

Jessy m Edmund Potter
1801-1891   1802-1883

Rupert Potter m Helen Leach
1832-1914   1839-1932

Helen Beatrix m William Heelis
1866-1943